Sweat of the Sun

GOLD OF PERU · ORO DEL PERU

CATALOGUE OF AN EXHIBITION
OF PERUVIAN TREASURES

CITY OF EDINBURGH ART CENTRE
1 AUGUST - 30 SEPTEMBER 1990

CITY OF EDINBURGH MUSEUMS AND ART GALLERIES
ISBN 0 905072 38 3

CONTENTS

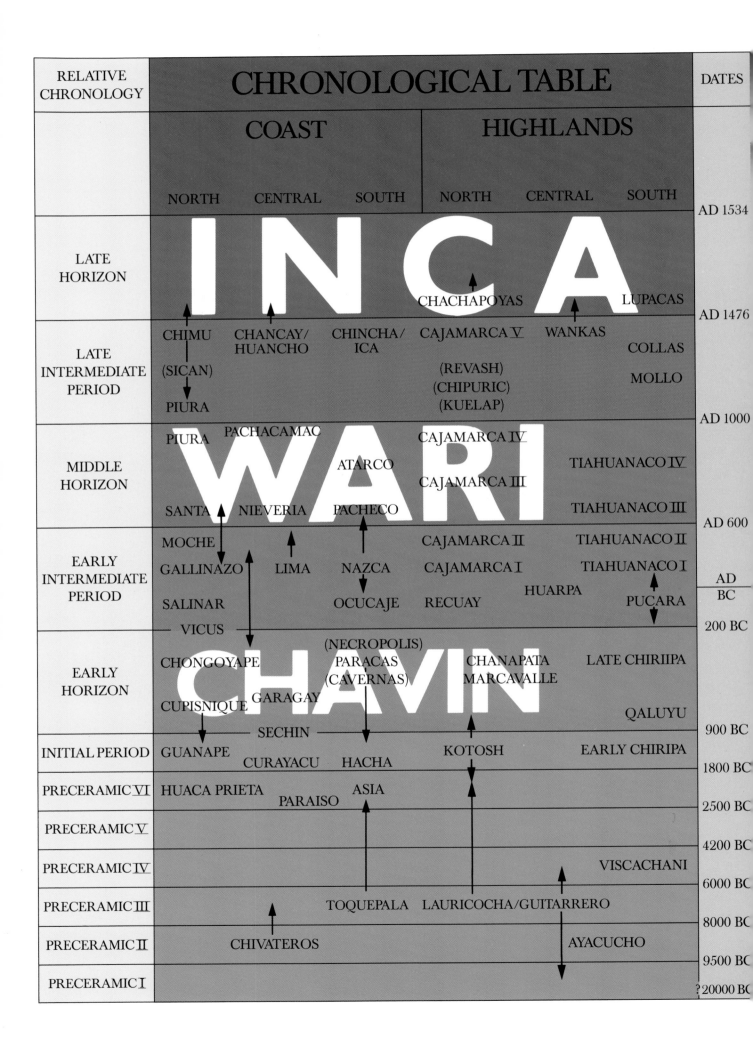

CHRONOLOGICAL TABLE

RELATIVE CHRONOLOGY	COAST			HIGHLANDS			DATES
	NORTH	CENTRAL	SOUTH	NORTH	CENTRAL	SOUTH	AD 1534
LATE HORIZON				CHACHAPOYAS		LUPACAS	AD 1476
LATE INTERMEDIATE PERIOD	CHIMU (SICAN) ↓ PIURA	CHANCAY/ HUANCHO	CHINCHA/ ICA	CAJAMARCA V (REVASH) (CHIPURIC) (KUELAP)	WANKAS	COLLAS MOLLO	AD 1000
MIDDLE HORIZON	PIURA SANTA	PACHACAMAC NIEVERIA	ATARCO PACHECO	CAJAMARCA IV CAJAMARCA III		TIAHUANACO IV TIAHUANACO III	AD 600
EARLY INTERMEDIATE PERIOD	MOCHE GALLINAZO SALINAR VICUS	LIMA	NAZCA OCUCAJE	CAJAMARCA II CAJAMARCA I RECUAY	HUARPA	TIAHUANACO II TIAHUANACO I PUCARA	AD / BC 200 BC
EARLY HORIZON	CHONGOYAPE CUPISNIQUE	GARAGAY	(NECROPOLIS) PARACAS (CAVERNAS) SECHIN	CHANAPATA MARCAVALLE		LATE CHIRIIPA QALUYU	900 BC
INITIAL PERIOD	GUANAPE	CURAYACU	HACHA	KOTOSH		EARLY CHIRIPA	1800 BC
PRECERAMIC VI	HUACA PRIETA	PARAISO	ASIA				2500 BC
PRECERAMIC V							4200 BC
PRECERAMIC IV						VISCACHANI	6000 BC
PRECERAMIC III		CHIVATEROS	TOQUEPALA	LAURICOCHA/GUITARRERO			8000 BC
PRECERAMIC II		CHIVATEROS			AYACUCHO		9500 BC
PRECERAMIC I							? 20000 BC

INCA WARI CHAVIN

COLOMBIA

EQUATOR

Quito

ECUADOR

Valdivia

Ingapirca

Tomebamba

Puná Island

Gulf of Guayaquil

Tumbes

Amazon

Frias

Vicus

SECHURA
DESERT

Huallaga River

Ucayali River

BRAZIL

Batan Grande

Pampa Grande

Kuelap

Cupisnique

Lambayeque

Cajamarca

Pacatnamu

PERU

Huaca Prieta

Macabi Island

La Galgada

Marañón River

Chan Chan

Moche

Pánamarca

Chavin de Huantar

Sechin

Huánuco Pampa

Recuay

Kotosh

PACIFIC
OCEAN

Lauricocha Cave

Chancay

Ancón

Jauja

Urubamba

El Paraiso

Lima

River

Machu Picchu

BOLIVIA

Pachacamac

Asia

Wari

Ollantaytambo

Pisac

Vilcashuamán

Cuzco

Piquillacta

Paracas

Raqchi

Cahuachi

Nazca

Pucará

Lake Titicaca

Sillustani

Tiahuanaco

Toquepala

BOLIVIA

Lake Poopó

CHILE

ATACAMA
DESERT

San Pedro de Atacama

Humahuaca

TROPIC OF CAPRICORN

FOREWORD

The Museo "Oro del Perú" ("Gold of Peru") Museum is a monument to the devoted and unceasing efforts of Miguel Mujica Gallo. Over a period of more than 40 years, he has assembled a collection of in excess of 15,000 pieces, which is representative of all the pre- Hispanic Peruvian cultures and, as well as metal artifacts, includes ceramics and textiles. In building his collection, it has been my father's objective to save important treasures from being removed from Peru forever, or from being melted down by unscrupulous metal merchants.

In order that Peru's cultural heritage might be better known internationally, for the last 30 years the Museo "Oro del Perú" has taken selections of its best pieces to the great cities of the world. This policy has been pursued because Peru's extraordinary pre-Hispanic artistic florescence must not be considered as only belonging to one nation, or continent, but should be seen as part of the cultural inheritance of all of mankind. In this connection, it has long been our hope to bring an exhibition to Edinburgh, the historic capital of Scotland, and I wish to thank all those who have worked to make this possible.

At the time of their conquest of Peru, in accord with the practices of the period, the Spanish seized many objects of precious metals, some of which had adorned temples and royal palaces, only to melt them down. This represented an immeasurable loss to art and archaeology. The items included in this exhibition survived because they were grave goods, interred with the dead only to be discovered centuries later. They represent the major cultures of pre-Hispanic Peru. Although up to the present many items have been recovered from the ground, it seems likely that much still remains hidden.

The works on display are manifestations of symbolic, dream and religious art. They are the products of a suite of sophisticated metallurgical techniques. Many were originally used to adorn fierce warriors, haughty monarchs or venerable priests. Others were made specifically for burial with the dead, funerary practices being of great importance to pre-Hispanic cultures. Hence their fragility and the unusual nature of their manufacture.

From earliest times, pre-Hispanic art appears to have invested gold with special symbolic significance. All of Peru's metal-making, prehistoric cultures expressed religious and ritual values through its use. Truly, it was the metal of the gods! The mounting of this exhibition in Edinburgh gives us great satisfaction. It is our sincere hope that it will serve to foster the ties of friendship and mutual understanding which already exist between Peru and Scotland.

VICTORIA MUJICA DE PEREZ PALACIO
Directora
Museo "Oro del Perú"

Sweat of the Sun

GOLD OF PERU · ORO DEL PERU

METALWORK IN PREHISPANIC PERU

The Central Andean region, from Ecuador to Bolivia, was the homeland of one of the world's great metallurgical traditions, one that developed independently without any contact or stimulus from Eurasia. During the first millennium B.C., knowledge of metalworking spread outwards from the centre of discovery in Peru and Bolivia, south into Chile and Argentina, and also northwards, to reach Colombia, Panama and Costa Rica around the time of Christ and Mexico by the 9th century A.D.

At the time of the Spanish Conquest the Central Andean metallurgical tradition had been in existence for well over two thousand years. During this long period, new alloys and techniques of manufacture were incorporated into the repertoire, regional styles emerged and then disappeared again, and political empires rose and fell. But underlying all these changes is an essential continuity. Certain metal forms such as *tupus* (garment pins), *tumis* (transverse knives), face masks and tubular earspools with frontal discs, are distinctively Andean and, in one style or another, remained popular for more than a thousand years. Other characteristic Andean traits are the custom of adding painted decoration to the surfaces of metal items, and a liking for inlays and mosaic work of coloured stone or shell. This taste for combining gold and silver with other precious materials is virtually absent outside the frontiers of the Inca empire.

Above all, however, continuity is reflected in technology, and in cultural attitudes towards the metals themselves and to the ways in which the raw materials should be used. In contrast to areas farther north (where small, delicate castings predominate), Peruvian smiths showed a strong preference for shaping metal items by hammering. Most objects, regardless of function or age, are worked to shape. Everyday tools of copper and bronze were cold-worked and annealed, or else were hot-forged. The jewellery metals (gold, silver and a wide variety of alloys) were beaten into sheet whose evenness and regularity compares with modern factory products. This sheet metal was then cut into shape, bent and rolled as required, pressed over or into moulds to produce sets of identical items, and then further decorated by embossing, incising or tracing designs onto the surface (Tushingham et al.1979; Bray 1972, 1985).

Sheet metal lends itself to the production of large, showy objects (masks, crowns, diadems, breastplates, ceremonial regalia, dishes and cups), but the same technology was used also for small items like figurines, delicate beads, nose-ornaments, pins and finger rings. Many of these ornaments are built up from pre-formed pieces of sheet metal which are joined mechanically (by folding, crimping, lacing and stapling, the use of tabs and slots) or metallurgically by means of soldering or welding. To the basic forms, Peruvian jewellers then added free-hanging sequins or danglers which shimmered and caught the light at the slightest movement.

As Lechtman has noted (1988:344), metal is treated as solid, not as liquid, and objects are 'constructed' rather than sculptured or modelled. This preference for sheet metal is culturally conditioned and is not inherent in the properties of the alloys themselves. Nor is it due to any lack of knowledge of the alternatives. When they wanted to do so, Andean metalsmiths showed competence in all the basic techniques of casting, and we must keep in mind that even sheet items were made from ingots of melted, and frequently alloyed, metal.

Even in their casting, however, the Peruvians were idiosyncratic. By contrast with the rest of the New World, in Peru the preferred method of casting was in

1. *Gold* tumi *with open-work decoration. Chimú. Cat. No. 198*

moulds. Open moulds, or basic two-piece moulds, were used for uncomplicated tools such as axes, chisels, hoes, maces etc. made of copper and its alloys. For more complex and three-dimensional forms, notably the solid figurines of the Inca period, multi-piece moulds were employed.

This use of moulds in pre-Hispanic America is very rare outside the Andean world. Farther north, from Colombia to Mexico, the usual technique was *cire perdue* casting, in which the smith began by making a wax model of the desired object. Over the wax model were brushed layers of semi-liquid clay, and the whole object was enveloped in a thick and porous casing of clay, or of clay mixed with charcoal. A channel was left through the casing so that, when everything was heated, the molten wax could be poured out. While the casing was still hot from the brazier, molten metal was poured in to take the place of the wax. After cooling, the outer casing was broken open to extract the finished article, an exact metal replica of the wax original. Lost wax castings of this kind are scarce in Peru perhaps because suitable wax was hard to obtain as the stingless American bee is not native to the Andes or the Pacific coast valleys (Bird 1979). Nevertheless, the technology was known to Moche smiths of the early centuries A.D., and was used extensively for ceremonial staff heads and copper ornaments during the centuries just before the Inca conquest.

Peruvian metallurgy is remarkable, above all, for its sophisticated use of alloys (Lechtman 1984, 1988). Iron was unknown in pre-European America but gold, silver, copper, tin and lead were in common use. Copper, alone or alloyed, was the metal of the common people, and was used for agricultural tools, needles, tweezers, axes, weapons and cheap trinkets. Unlike gold and silver, the manufacture of copper was probably not part of a state monopoly, and workshop zones with moulds, scrap metal, furnaces and manufacturing debris have been unearthed at archaeological sites throughout the Andes.

In the history of Peruvian metallurgy, two different copper alloys are of fundamental importance. In the southern Andean region true bronze (a copper-tin alloy) was in regular use by A.D. 600. The alloying element, tin, was readily available in the form of cassiterite (the oxide of that metal) in southern Peru, northern Bolivia and adjacent Argentina, both as placer deposits and in the form of veins. Analyses suggest that the cassiterite was smelted to produce metallic tin, which was then melted with copper metal to form bronze. High-tin bronze (generally with 10% to 13% tin) was used for casting, taking advantage of its superior strength and castability. Low-tin bronze (containing ca. 5% of tin) is more ductile and is easily worked cold, without becoming brittle; it was therefore preferred for sheet metal and for objects that were hammered and worked to shape.

In the northern Andes, where there are only minor sources of tin, a second alloy (copper-arsenic bronze) was developed during the early centuries A.D. and was in use on an industrial scale from about 900 until the Inca conquest of this area. The alloy has an attractive golden colour, can

be cast, and is also excellent for forging; it is durable, readily cold-worked with some annealing, and is as hard as tin-bronze. In the north it became the standard material for everday tools and household objects, but it was seldom used for large sheet metal items and was never the major jewellery alloy.

One of the pre-eminent characteristics of Andean metallurgy is a concern with *surfaces*, as well as with pure form (Lechtman 1988). Sheet metal items provide large surfaces for display, and alloys were selected to simultaneously exploit both their mechanical properties and their colour values. In Peru the production of silver has always outstripped that of gold, and silver was used as a metal in its own right and also as a component of alloys with gold and/or copper. The various combinations of these three metals provide a wide range of technical and aesthetic possibilities.

Copper-silver alloy is documented in the archaeological record as early as 700 B.C. and was commonly used from the Moche period until the Spanish Conquest. This alloy makes a good solder, and is tough and strong when hammered into sheet. In alloys containing as little as 10% of silver, the process of repeated hammering and annealing (bringing up to red heat) removes much of the surface copper through oxidation, leaving a bright silver colour. On analysis most large 'silver' items in ancient Peru turn out to be made from copper-silver alloy.

Copper-gold alloy (or *tumbaga*) becomes hard with hammering, but retains its flexibility and is well suited to sheet work. Alloys of these two metals make good solders and weld metals. Different variations in the degrees of redness of the metals can be produced by varying the copper content, and tumbaga articles can be given a golden surface by the process of depletion gilding (see below). Since gold often contains silver as a natural impurity, tumbaga alloys grade into true ternary alloys in which silver is deliberately added to gold and copper. The resultant alloy is a deep pink when cast, but can be manipulated to produce surfaces of a golden or silver colour. The pale yellow, or even greenish yellow, tone of much Peruvian jewellery comes from the presence of silver. By juggling with the metal composition and surface treatment, a wide range of 'gold' colours could be obtained.

Although Peruvian metalworkers were well aware of the mechanical properties of alloys, what gives central Andean metallurgy its individual quality is a set of *cultural* attitudes. As Lechtman (1988: 369-70) has commented:

In the Andes, metals carried and displayed the content or message of status, wealth and political power and reinforced the effective power of religious objects... From the earliest involvement of Andean peoples with metal up to the time of the Spanish conquest of the Inca empire, the two colors that were paramount in the metallurgical spectrum were gold and silver... Once color became the focus of property development, we are dealing with the metallurgy of surfaces, because the color of a metal object resides in its surface. The object may have one color at the surface and a totally different color underneath.

Peruvian metallurgy was, therefore, a metallurgy of surface transformation.

Many Peruvian items which appear at first sight to be made of gold are, in fact, of base metals or alloys enriched at the surfaces by some kind of gilding process. Techniques of gilding can be divided into two major categories: (1) those (e.g. foil gilding, fusion gilding, plating) which deposit a layer of gold onto a metal surface of any composition whatsoever, and (2) depletion gilding, effective only with alloys already containing gold, which works by removing the less noble metals at the surface of the object while leaving the gold unaffected.

Within the first category the most straightforward technique is foil gilding, in which a thin, malleable sheet of gold is mechanically attached to a substrate of another material. Once the foil is in place the entire piece may be heated so that interalloying takes place at the interface between the two metals, to produce a strong and permanent bond.

Fusion gilding, or wash gilding, is a more complex process by which molten metal (usually a gold or silver alloy with a relatively low melting temperature) is applied to the cleaned surface of an object made of copper or copper-rich alloy (Bergsøe 1936; Lechtman 1971; Scott 1986). If the ornament is to be coated all over it can be dipped into a bath of molten gold; if only one surface is to be treated the coating has to be flushed-on by hand. In either case, a firm bond is formed and the surfaces can be further enriched by depletion gilding to remove any unwanted copper. Fusion gilding is rare in Peru; it requires a precise control over alloys and their melting points, and is wasteful of gold by comparison with depletion

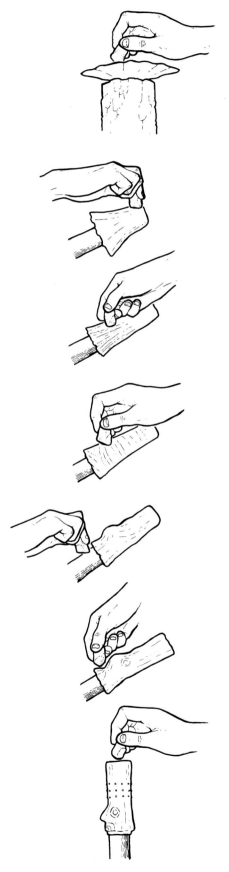

5. *Steps followed in hammering out an effigy beaker.*

gilding. Where this technique was invented is still unknown. It was used for both gilding and silvering in coastal Ecuador before the Inca expansion, and in Peru may have been employed by Vicús and Moche metalsmiths.

It was this Moche-Vicús metalwork that provided a major surprise in the mid-1970s. While examining a group of corroded sheet copper articles from Loma Negra, researchers from the Massachusetts Institute of Technology noticed that the copper had originally been covered with a coating of gold or silver, so thin and regular that it resembled modern electroplating (Lechtman et al. 1982; Lechtman 1984b). Analysis suggested that the effect was achieved by a technique of electrochemical replacement plating, making use of solutions containing a mixture of corrosive minerals available to Andean metalsmiths, but requiring no external source of electrical current.

All the above methods of gilding rely on the deposition of a layer of gold onto an item made of a different metal. Depletion gilding, however, works on a diametrically opposed principle, not the addition of new material, but the removal of unwanted base metals from the surface of an alloy already containing gold.

Lechtman (1971, 1973) has studied the techniques used in north Peru to produce golden surfaces on objects made of a copper-silver alloy containing a percentage of gold. During the process of hammering and annealing the sheet metal, a copper oxide scale formed on the surface of the object and was removed with a mild acid pickle. This reduction of the copper content left a silver-coloured surface layer, containing some gold as a minor constituent. The next stage involved the selective removal of the silver, to leave a gold-rich, 'depletion gilded' surface. This can be achieved by a process akin to cementation (for instance, by heating the alloy in a crucible packed with salt and clay dust moistened with urine) or by using an acid bath. Since the ancient Peruvians had no distilled acids, they must have used a solution containing one of the corrosive minerals (such as ferric sulphate or cupric sulphate), which are abundant in the coastal desert. Dissolved in water, with the addition of salt or alum, these minerals are capable of removing both copper and silver to leave a gold-rich surface. The quality and thickness of the gold layer depends on the temperature and duration of the treatment, as well as on the strength of the acid mixture. The method works well for ternary alloys high in silver, and also for tumbaga alloys. Laboratory experiments show that alloys with as little as 12% gold can be depletion gilded.

Choice of alloys and of surface treatment allowed metalsmiths to produce a range of hues within the categories 'gold' or 'silver', and to combine these into bimetallic items of contrasting colours. All these techniques were fully developed on the north coast of Peru a thousand years before the rise of the Inca empire.

6. *Moche form, with separate arms, used in the production of sheet-metal figures.*

7. *One of a pair of richly ornamented silver earspools. Moche. Cat. No. 63.*

STYLISTIC AND AESTHETIC DEVELOPMENTS IN PERUVIAN METALWORK.

8. *Gold earspool centrepiece, ornamented with zoomorphic figure with feline attributes. Chavín. Cat. No. 2.*

Although we can talk of a distinctively Andean tradition of metalworking, this was neither uniform nor unchanging. Aesthetic preferences were subject to fashion, and local styles of metalworking emerged in the various regions of Peru. This section looks at the development of central Andean metallurgy in its historical and cultural context.

1. The first Peruvian metalwork: the Initial Period and the Early Horizon.

By comparison with the Old World, metallurgy was late to develop in the Americas. The most ancient evidence for metalworking anywhere in Latin America comes from the site of Waywaka, in the south-central Peruvian highlands, where Grossman (1972) discovered tiny fragments of gold foil dating to ca. 1500 B.C. In the same excavation he found a goldworker's tool kit consisting of three cylindrical stone hammers and a mushroom-shaped stone anvil. Without analysis, we cannot say whether these scraps of foil were hammered from naturally occurring nuggets or from ingots of melted gold.

Waywaka is an isolated discovery, and we have no adequate sample of metalwork until the Chavín period several centuries later. Almost all Chavín metal objects come from rich tombs at Chongoyape in the Lambayeque valley (Lothrop 1941), an unknown site somewhere in the north highlands (Lothrop 1951), and Kuntur Wasi in Cajamarca (Carrión Cachot 1948; Onuki 1989). Taken together, the finds from these three localities define the Chavín jewellery style. All the pieces are luxury items made from hammered sheet: crowns, diadems, nose-ornaments, ear spools, beads, gorgets, pins, spoons and tweezers for removing facial hair. Many of these articles are decorated with the characteristic motifs of Chavín art (stylized jaguars, serpents, mythical beings), and several items still have traces of red or black paint.

Sheet metal was cut out, bent and rolled, embossed and pressed into shape. Three dimensional human and animal figures were made by joining pre-prepared components, and some of these items were bimetallic. One of the finest pieces in this category is a gold spoon topped by a hollow, squatting human figure (containing a rattle pellet) who is blowing into a conch shell trumpet made of silver (Lothrop 1951, Fig.77b).

The few analyses of Chavín metalwork are published by Lothrop (1951). Three specimens - a bead, a little crab and a piece of sheet - were of pure gold. A pin head from Chongoyape proved to be of silver with 26% gold, and certain objects from the highlands were of gold with a good deal of silver and a little copper. Copper wire of Chavín age or earlier is reported from Pacopampa (Fung 1975:186) and a copper disc, perhaps gilded, from Puémape (Elera Arevalo 1989). Finally, there is a bead of surface-enriched copper- silver alloy from Malpaso, in the Lurín valley of the central coast, with a date of ca. 700 B.C. (Lechtman 1979:26).

We have no information about the non-funerary aspects of Chavin metalworking, but by the end of the Early Horizon the key traits of the Andean sheet metal tradition had already made their appearance. Casting may also have been employed, if a cast silver feline in the Museo Nacional, Lima, is correctly attributed to this period (Pimentel Gurmendi 1981:7).

2. The Early Intermediate Period

This is a time when Peruvian territory was divided among a number of regional states, each of which had its own political sphere of influence and its own art style.

a. The north coast: Gallinazo, Moche and Vicús

In this area the local Chavín style was followed successively by Salinar and Gallinazo materials. Salinar sites have yielded no significant metalwork, but from the Gallinazo phase we have, for the first time, a substantial quantity of copper (some of it gilded) as well as gold and silver. These items also include everyday objects such as tweezers, pins, wire, bangles, beads and a knife.

With the development of the Moche empire (ca. 200 B.C. - A.D. 700), metal becomes abundant in the archaeological record. Jones (1979) has reviewed the older discoveries. They include many kinds of objects illustrated in the painted or modelled scenes on Moche pottery; headdress ornaments with the face of the Fanged God, sheet metal turban pieces in the shape of fox heads, and also nose ornaments, back plates, rattles, pedestalled cups, and a magnificent series of ear spools inlaid with stone and shell mosaic. The figurative items depict the familiar themes of Moche art: warriors with slings or darts, figures in procession, decapitation scenes and trophy heads, owls and birds of prey, lizards and dragon monsters. Figures in the round were made by joining sheet metal parts shaped over wooden or copper models. Copper chisels were topped with miniature sculptured scenes, made by casting, which depict bound prisoners, human beings and deity figures.

Metal was by now cheap enough to appear in the tombs of ordinary men and women (Donnan and Mackey 1978). Corpses were interred with their ear plugs and depilatory tweezers, with copper masks or discs over their faces, and scraps of copper placed in their hands and mouths.

Very rich Moche burials are mentioned in Colonial documents (and in 1602 more

than 2700 kilos of gold was looted from the main platform at Moche itself), but it was not until 1987 that archaeologists were able to excavate an untouched royal tomb, at the Huaca Rajada, near Sipán in the Lambayeque valley (Alva 1988, 1990). The quantity and quality of the funerary offerings are extraordinary. The principal burial was accompanied by feather ornaments, shrouds, banners and clothing sewn with metal plaques, golden headdress ornaments, bells, back plates and minor items. The corpse was festooned with gold, silver and copper objects. Ear spools of gold and mosaic lay beside the head; over the lower part of his face was a gold mask, and his nose and eyes were covered with sheet gold; turquoise and gold bracelets adorned his arms; ingots of gold and copper lay in his hands; on his feet were ceremonial gold sandals. Some of the items from the Huaca Rajada mausoleum belong to well known Moche categories, but others (like the necklaces of gold and silver peanuts or the snarling faces of gilded copper) are unique to this site.

The term Vicús is applied to material from cemeteries of shaft-and-chamber tombs at various sites in the upper Piura valley, in the far north of Peru. This culture was unknown until the 1960s, when large quantities of pottery and metalwork began to appear on the art market (Disselhof 1971, 1972; Lumbreras 1979). Some of the vessels were in distinct local style; others were pure Moche, from all the substages of this style (Shimada 1987:133).

In 1969 a new Vicús cemetery, with several hundred tombs, was discovered at Loma Negra. A single grave contained almost 100 metal pieces, and the total sample from Loma Negra consists of more than 700 items: nose ornaments, finials, pendants and - unique to the Vicús area - a series of cut-out discs and crescentic plaques topped by cut-out figures. Most of the objects are of sheet metal,

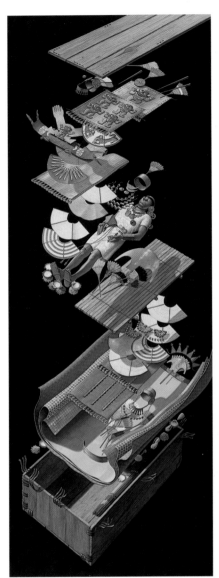

9. *Burial riches of Moche royal tomb at Sipán. Painting by Ned Seidler. (By courtesy of the National Geographic Society.)*

10. *Gold and silver nose ornament. Vicús. Cat. No. 25.*

predominantly copper, and often have gold or silver surfaces. Several categories occur as pairs or in matching sets, and the blue-green corrosion that covers their surfaces has preserved impressions of the textiles in which the items were wrapped for burial (Schaffer 1986).

The designs on this metalwork represent carefully selected themes drawn from Moche ritual and mythology. Schaffer (1981, 1983) has identified the Moche Fanged God and a range of monster-headed creatures, including the crested dragon-like Moon Animal (Bruhns 1976) and demonic beings with human or snake bodies. These figures appear in scenes showing the capture of prisoners, human sacrifice, and decapitation, with condors pecking at corpses and trophy heads. The style is pure Moche, but the subject matter shows a distinct regional emphasis.

Recent investigations have revealed the first metal-production sites in the Vicús region. A clay furnace at Pampa Juarez, with hearths, fire pits and copper slag, gave a radiocarbon date of A.D. 210 ± 65 years (Kaulicke 1988/9), and workshops with hammers, anvils and part-finished items have been found at this site and at Loma Valverde (Shimada 1988/9). The relationship between the local people and the Moche component in Vicús is still far from clear, but some scholars believe the metalwork was produced by a closely supervised colony of Moche artisans working in foreign territory far from their coastal homeland (Shimada 1987).

b. The north highlands: Recuay

Although the Recuay and Moche cultures were broadly contemporary, and shared a common frontier, the two metal styles are quite different. Recuay metalwork is represented by the content of a rich tomb at Pashash (Grieder 1978), with copper, or copper alloy, bells, nails, ear spools, wire and sheathing, a gold bell in the shape of a human head, and a remarkable series of copper pins with forged shafts ending in cast, drum-shaped heads. On the heads of these pins were the typical motifs of the Recuay style: human figures, owls, felines, and the crested Moon Animal. Some pins had once been covered in gold foil; others had coloured stone inlays and cloisonné work. Recuay jewellery has no obvious antecedents and seems to have had no influence on the styles of neighbouring territories. It exists, for the moment, in isolation.

c. The south coast: Nazca

There is very little metalwork from the Early Horizon in the south coast valleys, but with the emergence of the Nazca culture around 200 B.C. metal items become more plentiful and spectacular (Lothrop 1937). Most of these objects are from mummy bundles; each bundle contains the possessions of a single individual, and gives some indication of the jewellery which he or she wore during life.

11. *Sheet-gold mouth ornament. Nazca. Cat. No. 156.*

In the Early Nazca necropolis at Wari Kayan, Mummy No. 310 was buried with 2 diadems, discs for each ear, 2 bracelets, strips of sheet gold on the cheeks, a folded hemisphere of gold, and a few miscellaneous bits of sheet metal. A rolled up sheet of gold was in the mouth of the corpse, and another had once blocked the anus. (Tello and Mejia Xesspe 1979: 381-2). Inside another bundle (No. 253) at the same site, a little cloth package lay close to the body and contained sixteen miniature items of sheet metal: discs, nose-ornaments, diadems and bracelets (op.cit: 436).

The best Nazca ornaments are of highly polished sheet gold, and are often of large size. The range of variety is limited; the most typical items are turban decorations, diadems embossed with human or monster faces, and the well-known mouth masks with lateral appendages in the form of snakes or humming birds. On Nazca pottery these same ornaments are depicted, worn by human figures and also by composite mythological creatures, some of whom carry trophy heads. It may be that gods and humans shared the same taste in jewellery, or, as Proulx (1983: 95) has suggested, that *'high status males,*

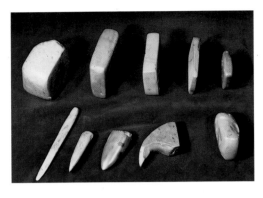

12. *Set of Peruvian metalworker's hammer-stones. Norfolk (Virginia) Museum of Arts and Sciences.*

probably priests, were at least partly dressed in the image of these mythical beings.'

Nazca metalwork illustrates, to an extreme degree, the Peruvian preference for hammering rather than casting, not only for parade items but also for miniature trophy head pendants and figurines (Lechtman 1988: 347,370). This emphasis is clearly a matter of choice rather than necessity; a number of cast spear-thrower pegs from the later stages of the Nazca sequence prove that alternative techniques were available.

3. The Middle Horizon

During this period much of Peru came under the influence of Wari, a highland city in the Ayacucho Basin. Pottery and other objects decorated in the Wari style began to appear on the south and central coasts of Peru, sometimes alone, sometimes accompanied by items made by the local people in their own regional fashions. In metalwork we can distinguish three groups of material during the Middle Horizon: (1) undiagnostic, everyday, objects such as *tupus,* needles and tools, made of copper and its alloys, (2) luxury objects, usually of gold or silver, with Wari designs, and (3) locally made metalwork in which Wari influence is absent or very slight.

Wari art is, above all, a religious art, and certain mythological figures occur wherever the style is spread. The principal figure is a personage with a square face (sometimes with tear-bands on his cheeks), from which emanate rays ending in dotted circles, animal heads or bird heads. This deity is sometimes attended by 'angels' (winged figures with bird or human faces) or accompanied by a feline creature with a ring-shaped nose.

Metal objects with this pure Wari iconography are surprisingly rare and none has been recorded from the capital itself, though the Moraduchayuq workshop area of the site yielded a thin sheet of gold from which a figure had been cut out and removed (Isbell 1984:117). A few isolated Wari pieces exist in collections

(e.g. Wardwell 1968: 28-9; Sawyer 1968: 66), but the only large documented find is a from a cemetery at Pomacanchi, near Cuzco, where metalworking furnaces have also been reported (Chavez 1987). The Pomacanchi collection includes some little cut out silhouettes made of gold, but most of the items seem to be of silvered sheet copper. The inventory includes bracelets or anklets, bells, strips or bands, part of a plaque, and a series of ornamental headdress plumes with representations of the square-faced Wari deity. On some of the plumes the design is produced by rocker stamping, a technique in which the engraving tool is 'walked' over the surface with a rocking movement, leaving a zigzag line. This technique is frequent in the Middle Horizon, but was soon abandoned.

Sheet items with Wari iconography occur sporadically in the main centres of Wari influence on the coasts, from Pinilla, in the Ica valley to the south (Paulsen 1969) to Pachacamac in the Lurín valley, and the Ancón cemetery on the central coast (Eisleb and Strelow 1980, nos. 301-306; Menzel 1977: 41-50).

The Wari religion found its greatest acceptance on the south coast, and there was a considerable merging between the final Nazca substyles of the coast and the Middle Horizon styles of the highlands. To this overlap period belong a series of gold cuffs with raised bosses, a few cross-shaped plaques in the shape of stylized birds, and also a group of seated burials wrapped in textiles and provided with artificial heads made of cloth. The facial area was covered with coloured feathers, and the features (eyes, nose, mouth, and cheek bands like those of the Wari deity) were reproduced in sheet metal and attached to the backing (Anton 1987: 74). A variant form of this idea is found too, in the other main area of Wari influence, the central coast (Katz 1983: 308-9; Menzel 1977: 41- 50).

With the decline of Wari influence after the fall of the capital, the coherence of the imposed religious iconography began to

13. *Gold funerary mask. Chimú. Cat. No. 191.*

break down in the outlying provinces, until, eventually, new regional styles of metalworking emerged. The archaeology of this period is still poorly understood.

4. The coastal styles of the Late Intermediate Period

The history of Peru between the fall of the Wari empire and the Inca conquest is complex, with political fragmentation which is reflected in the large number of regional art styles. Metal was in common use everywhere, but it is only in the coastal regions that we have large samples for study. Each sub-region has its own characteristics, but certain categories of artifacts (e.g. mummy masks made of sheet metal, beakers with straight, slightly flaring sides, drinking vessels with faces in high relief), are almost universal.

a. The south coast: Ica and Chincha

Although metal artifacts are numerous in the south coast valleys, few pieces are from scientific excavations. The Spanish chronicler Cieza de León commented that noble families were buried in special cemeteries with deep and elaborate tombs, and that the looted remains of these were still visible at the time of his travels in 1547-50. The general accuracy of Cieza's account is proved by a series of undisturbed tombs excavated by Max Uhle at Old Ica (Menzel 1976: 45, 1977: 8-18).

One of the tombs excavated by Uhle (No.Th-1) belonged to a nobleman of the Late Intermediate Period. The skeleton had a flake of gold in his mouth, and was buried with a golden death mask. Accompanying the body were his personal possessions: some 250 pottery vessels, a golden headband, a gold beaker with repoussé geometric ornament and another one with a human face in relief, gold sequins from a vanished textile, a pair of gold armlets and, in silver, various drinking cups, food dishes, finger rings and ear plugs.

When the Incas conquered the south coast, the local leaders were incorporated into the ranks of the Inca administration and, like senior officals everywhere in the Inca Empire, were permitted to use gold and silver. A second tomb excavated by Uhle (No. Td-8) is that of an Ica official under the Inca rule. The pottery from the burial chamber included local copies of Inca wares, and among the offerings were a wooden stool, wooden implements with gold and silver sheathing, weaving tools, sea shells, llama bones, a silver disc, and a conical plume holder made from hammered gold and with a human face in relief. Nine sacrificed youths (one of them with gold, silver and copper jewellery) were laid on the floor of the tomb, and fifteen red-painted human skulls were deposited higher up in the fill.

A third group of Ica metalwork, reported to come from a single tomb, was examined by Brown (1984). Her analyses showed that most of the objects were not of pure metal but of alloys, tumbaga and copper-gold-silver. The list of artifacts matches what was found in Uhle's tombs; face beakers and plume holders, tweezers, little hollow birds, ear discs, a mask with the usual Ica diamond-shaped eyes, and a number of minor objects. Several of the discs bore one of the most typical Ica designs - a plain bird standing out against a stippled background. This motif is found everywhere along the coast during the Late Intermediate Period, and is clearly related to the press-moulded designs of Chimú pottery far to the north.

b. The cultures of the central coast

The metalwork of this area has never been studied as a group. Spanish chronicles report that in pre-Inca times the valleys of the central coast from Huaura to Lurín formed a single political state, the kingdom of Cuismancu, but this unity is not reflected in the archaeology. The central coast seems to have been a transitional zone between north and south Peru, influenced by both, and without a strong metallurgical personality of its own. Metal artifacts are fairly abundant (Baessler 1906) but most of them have no background information. In consequence, it is often difficult to tell which objects were made on the central coast and which were imported from neighbouring regions, either by merchants or by pilgrims visiting the oracle at Pachacamac.

Southern connections are demonstrated by finds of face beakers, masks, and vessels identical to those described from Ica (Ríos and Retamozo 1978), and by the continuance into the Late Intermediate Period of mummy burials with false faces (de Lavalle and Lang 1982: 24-6; Menzel 1977: 45). On the northern frontier of Cuismancu, trade with the Chimú kingdom brought imported pottery, textiles and shells to the people of the Huaura and Chancay valleys. Metal objects also figured in this trade, and stylistic distinctions become blurred in this frontier region. Tombs containing offerings in both Chimú and Chancay styles (and some which could belong to either of these) are illustrated by Rowe (1984: 155-64).

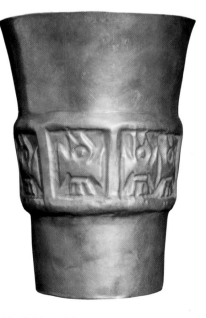

14. *Gold vessel decorated with stylised birds. Chimú. Cat. No. 182.*

The black and white effigy pots of Chancay show figures wearing disc-headed *tupu* pins, and the Chancay people were also fond of models and genre scenes, sometimes in cast metal but more often assembled from sheet. The repertoire includes birds and animals, musicians and miniature instruments, trees, and more complex scenes such as a tiny garden with a figure tending recognizable maize and manioc plants, or a funerary procession with bearers carrying a litter and a casket (Emmerich 1965: 40). These items are the strongest candidates for local manufacture; they are equivalents in metal of subjects modelled on Chancay pottery or represented by groups of Chancay cloth dolls engaged in weaving and other activities.

c. The north coast: Sicán and Chimú
When the Inca armies invaded northen Peru they came into conflict with the powerful Chimú (or Chimor) kingdom, which controlled the coastal lands from the Ecuadorian frontier to the Rímac valley, just north of Lima. All the Late and Intermediate metalwork of this vast area was uncritically labelled 'Chimú', and it was not until the 1980s that archaeologists recognised two separate, but parallel, artistic traditions on the north coast: *Middle Sicán* (centred on the Lambayeque valley between A.D. 800 and 1100), and *Chimú* proper (associated with the Chimor empire and its capital at Chan Chan in the Moche valley). The two styles share several elements of technology and iconography. Many items cannot be attributed to one or the other, and could have been made anywhere on the north coast. There is, however, one cluster of metal objects (including some of Peru's most famous gold and silver treasures) which undoubtedly came from Sicán workshops.

The characteristic Sicán products include metal vessels copying the shapes of Lambayeque bridge-spouted or stirrup-spouted pots, a group of large ceremonial *tumis* topped by figures wearing crescent headdresses, beakers with flaring sides, embossed with figures or with geometric designs, or inlaid with coloured stones, and, finally, a splendid series of mummy masks in sheet gold or gold alloy (Carcedo Muro and Shimada 1985). The most notable feature of Middle Sicán metalwork is the ubiquitous presence of a deity known as the Sicán Lord. The iconography never varies. He is depicted with a rectangular face and a curved, rounded jawline; the eyes are comma shaped and pointed at the outer

15. *Gold beaker ornamented with inverted anthropomorphic faces on either side. Traces of paint remain. Chimú. Cat. No. 171.*

edges; he wears an elaborate crescentic headdress, and has tab-like rectangular ears with large circular ornaments in the lobes.

Many Sicán objects, in particular the masks, have futher decoration - the eyes are inlaid or provided with 'tears' made of lapis lazuli, emeralds or gold spheres; faces are painted with zones of red, green or white; some masks still show traces of mosaic patterns of coloured feathers, and other examples may have had feather panaches attached to the upper edges. At this point we must stop thinking in terms of gold and silver alone, and must consider Sicán masks as multimedia works of art.

Most of the Middle Sicán pieces in museums and collections come from rich tombs at Batán Grande (Lambayeque). The contents of some of these are listed by Carcedo Muro and Shimada (1985). A single grave from the platform of Huaca El Corte, looted in the 1950s, contained more than 200 gold and silver objects in pure Sicán style, of which 176 were beakers. Another tomb, from Huaca Menor at Batán Grande, contained a more representative selection of artifacts: mantles decorated with red shell, lapis lazuli and cinnabar, wooden sceptres and arrow shafts, at least one blackware effigy pot, a quartz necklace, great quantities of gold foil, and an estimated 500 kg. of copper tools, including stacks of *naipes* (thin copper plaques of standardised shapes and weights, which may have served as money-ingots in commercial transactions). This find demonstrates that we cannot separate copper metallurgy from that of silver and gold.

Copper was the basic raw material for tools, but it also was used for the alloys from which prestige items were made. Copper oxide ores from the local mines in the Lambayque area were transported to smelting sites where they were mixed with arsenic-bearing sulphide ores, probably brought in from the highlands of Cajamarca, some 120 km away. At smelting sites like Huaca del Pueblo Batán Grande (Middle Sicán) and Cerro Huaringa (Late Sicán) the excavators found sets of furnaces and all the debris of smelting: fragments of slag, ores and flux minerals, charges, and ceramic blowtube tips or *tuyeres*. Arsenic-bronze was used on a small scale for jewellery in the Moche period, but at the start of the Middle Sicán period it became the standard material for tools particularly cast agricultural tools. Production reached truly industrial levels. From the smelters, most of the ingots passed to workshops in the cities, where some of the metal was used directly for tools and the rest alloyed with gold or silver for the jewellery tools. Production was on an industrial scale, many of the copper tools in the Batán Grande tombs were poorly made, or even unused, and may have represented stocks of metallic wealth rather than implements for everyday work.

During the century between ca. 1350 and 1450, the kingdom of Chimor conquered its neighbours and reached its maximum extent. The Lambayeque valley was overrun, the characteristic Sicán items ceased to be made, and the Chimú style came to dominate the entire north coast. Thousands of presumed Chimú metal artifacts exist in collections all over the world, but only a handful of pieces were excavated by archaeologists. Provenences are vague, attributions dubious, grave lots have been split up, and few items can be accurately dated.

Antze (1965) and Reichlen (1941) illustrate a good selection of minor objects, and Emmerich (1965, Fig. 29) illustrates a complete set of noblemen's ornaments made of beaten gold: a tall crown with four golden plumes, a pair of ear spools ending in discs nearly 12 cm in diameter, a necklace of spherical beads, and a wide collar decorated with repoussé human figures and fringed with a row of pendant plaques. From collections in Peru come metal cuirasses, woven ponchos and cloth bags sewn with metal plaques, standards, gauntlets, carved wooden litters with gold overlay, ceremonial items, and vessels for eating and drinking (Tushingham et al. 1979; Moseley 1978).

Chimú workmanship is seen at its best on the sheet metal ear spools in the form of long cylinders with large disc-shaped heads. Around the cylinders are miniature engraved scenes which can be matched at a larger scale on Chimú pottery and architectural friezes: heads with beaky noses and tassel headdresses, human figures, birds, animals and fishermen in reed boats. The frontal disc often depicts the most common Chimú icon, a human or divine personage with almond-shaped eyes, wearing a crescent headdress, and sometimes flanked by attendants or riding in a litter. This figure is universal in Chimú art, and is found also on pottery, wooden objects and textiles (Howe 1984).

In metalwork the Chimú Lord appears on objects of all kinds. Sometimes the entire figure is embossed, but frequently it is built up from separately formed cut out and embossed sheet metal elements, stapled and soldered together. First the body was created, with limbs feet and hands. Already the figure is partly in the round: the face is curved, the feet project forward, the arms are free. The poncho and headdress were then added; objects were placed in the hands, and there may be a free-hanging mask over the face; subsidiary figures may finally be added to the composition.

These Chimú pieces illustrate the relationship between techniques of manufacture and aesthetic values. Outside Peru, any objects as three-dimensional as the Chimú Lord would have been cast in a single piece. To a European eye, expecting naturalistic modelling (easy to achieve by casting), a Chimú figure looks crude and 'unreal', like a child's cardboard cutout - and yet, the Chimú figure has a logic of its own. The layering technique gives a sense of depth, of foreground and background, of overlap in space between one figure and another, of highlights and shadows.

5. Metallurgy in the Inca Empire

The expansion of the Inca state brought with it great changes. For the first time, all the coastal and Andean lands, from

16. *Gold and silver* tumi. *Ornamented with an anthropomorphic head inlaid with turquoise. Chimú. Cat. No. 197.*

Argentina and Chile in the south to Ecuador in the north, were brought under the control of a single government and formed part of a single economic system.

This control extended to the tin sources of Bolivia, and metallic tin from south of Lake Titicaca was transported all over the empire, to be alloyed to locally produced copper. Under the new economic system tin-bronze replaced the old arsenical coppers of the north, and certain standardized tool forms (e.g. star-shaped maces, axes with side lugs for lashing to a handle) became universal. Casting revived in popularity, especially for figurines and *tumi* handles, and metal-in-metal inlay was an Inca innovation. Animals, human figures, *tumis*, and votive axes were cast from silver or copper, with hollows or grooves where the inlay was to go; then strips of other metals were cut to shape and hammered or glued into place. Sometimes a coloured paste was used to fill the depression instead of metal. Wooden beakers were occasionally inlaid with lead.

One of the best documented collections of Inca metalwork comes from Hiram Bingham's excavations at Machu Picchu in 1911-12. This town was the centre of a royal estate belonging to the Inca ruler (Rowe 1987), and some of the inhabitants were metalsmiths. The finds include raw metal (both copper and tin), heavy tools (axes, chisels, bolas, plumb bobs) and a wide range of personal possessions: shawl pins, *tumis*, tweezers, sewing needles, ear ornaments, bracelets, finger rings and a necklace (Mathewson 1915; Routledge and Gordon 1987). The most common alloy was tin-bronze, but several items were made of silver-copper alloy and one unique spatula had a decorative head made of bismuth-bronze. Sheet metal objects were surprisingly rare, and most of the artifacts in the collection are either cast or forged.

The finds from Machu Picchu consist of everyday items belonging to Inca townspeople, who were not important enough to own gold and silver objects. Precious metals were reserved for the use of the ruler in Cuzco and for nobles to whom this privilege was expressly granted. All gold was taken by the government, which kept inspectors at the mining sites, and the raw metal was passed on to subsidized craftsmen who worked for the Inca himself or for client lords. The mestizo writer Garcilaso de la Vega commented in 1609 that when local rulers *(curacas)* visited the supreme Inca they would bring him *'men skilled in all these arts ..... as worthy to serve their king.'* (Root 1949: 209). The state, too, moved craftsmen from one region to another, transplanting Chimú metalworkers to Cuzco and Ica smiths to Cochabamba in Bolivia.

Colonial accounts of Inca mines and workshops are summarized in Root (1949) and Bray (1972). The most complete description of workshop practises comes from Garcilaso:

They used very hard stones, of a colour between green and yellow, instead of anvils ..... Nor could they make hammers with wooden handles. But they worked with certain instruments made of copper and brass mixed together. These tools were of the shape of dice with the corners rounded off. Some are large, so that the hand can just clasp them, others middling size, others small, and others lengthened out to hammer on a concave. They hold these hammers in their hands to strike with as if they were pebbles. They had no files or graving tools, nor had they invented the art of making bellows for blast furnaces. They blasted by means of tubes of copper ..... As many as 8, 10 or 12 of these were put together, according to the requirements of the furnace; and they went round the fire blowing with the tubes ..... They had no tongs for drawing the metal out from the fire, but did this with poles of wood or copper ..... They also found out, in spite of their simplicity, that the smoke of certain metals was injurious to the health, and they consequently made their foundries in the open air, in the yards and courts, and never under a roof. (Root 1949: 209-10).

Gold and silver and their alloys were used almost exclusively for luxury articles and ceremonial items: cups and vessels, pins and jewellery, sequins and danglers for sewing onto clothing, and also little genre scenes of human figures carrying chicha jars, herding llamas, or playing musical instruments. Unusually for Peru, these miniature figurines were solid cast, rather than assembled from sheet metal, and they are made with the aid of multi-piece moulds.

Gold and silver were intimately connected with power and status in the Inca world, and the ruler distributed gold and silver items to members of the nobility as a reward for administrative or military service to the state. Because precious metals were a state monopoly, aesthetic canons and design motifs were largely dictated by the political and religious bodies which commissioned the work and controlled its distribution (Lechtman 1977; Helms 1981; Moseley 1978). This resulted in what Moseley (1978: 18) has called a *'corporate style'*, associated with a particular political and religious ideology. The Inca aristocracy claimed divine descent from the sun, and the ruling Inca was in his lifetime semi-divine, the sun's representative on earth. This special creation gave the Inca state a god-given

17. *Small gold female and male figurines. Inca. Cat. Nos. 292-293.*

22

right to conquer and to civilize all lesser peoples. In reserving gold, the *'sweat of the sun'*, and silver, the *'tears of the moon'*, for his own use, the Inca was asserting the rights and status of the ruling class. This political ideology was designed to separate the Inca aristocracy from the common populace, and to perpetuate the Incas' image of themselves as a chosen people.

Given the relationship between the Inca state and its gods, it is predictable that gold and silver will be found abundantly in temples and shrines. Cieza de Léon comments that in all provincial capitals *'the kings had temples of the sun, and houses with great store of plate, with people whose only duty it was to work at making rich pieces of gold and great bars of silver.'* (Root 1949: 209). At Cuzco, the Coricancha (the *'court of Gold'*, where Viracocha and the heavenly bodies were worshipped) had an ornamental frieze of sheet gold almost a metre wide along the inner and outer walls, and the entrances were covered in gold plates. In the central patio was a fountain sheathed in gold, surrounded by a garden of maize plants made of sheet gold, with more than twenty life-sized gold llamas guarded by golden herdsmen. Inside the various sanctuaries of Coricancha were images of the sun and moon, and also the mummies of dead rulers, seated on chairs of gold placed upon golden slabs (Lothrop 1938). As the chronicler Huaman Poma put it, *'Anyone walking into that blaze of gold appeared like a corpse as his features took on the colour of the metal.'*

At the miniature end of the scale, among the most typical Inca metal items are the little human and llama figures made of gold and silver. Some of them are solid, but most are hammered from sheet metal and assembled from separate elements joined together. A llama figure in the Museum fur Volkerkunde, in Berlin, proved to be made from 13 pre-formed components (von Schuler 1972: 27). Human figures, male and female, were assembled in the same way, then dressed in miniature clothing, complete with mantles (and *tupu* pins to fasten them), feather headdresses and little coca bags.

Spanish chronicles indicate that these miniature figurines were used in the *capacocha* sacrifices, which took place during the celebration of the winter solstice, upon the death of an Inca ruler (or the anniversary of his death) and at the coronation of a new Inca. At sites all over the empire, pairs of young children, one of each sex, were buried alive, dressed in their best clothes and accompanied by household goods, gold and silver vessels, coloured *Spondylus* shells, and other precious items. At the summit of Cerro El Plomo, in north Chile, an Inca child sacrifice of just this kind was discovered, high above the snowline, and the offerings included miniature human and llama figures made of precious metals and *Spondylus* shell (Mostny 1957). Remains of similar *capacocha* offerings have been found on several volcanic peaks on the southern frontier of the empire (Beorchia Nigris 1984) and, at the northern edge of Inca territory, on La Plata Island off the coast of Ecuador (McEwan and Silva 1989). Figurines are also reported from some of the major imperial shrines, the Island of the Sun in Lake Titicaca, Pachacamac on the central coast, and from the Coricancha itself in Cuzco.

At the time of European contact, the quantity of precious metal in the Inca Empire was impressive. Cieza de León, writing between 1532 and 1550, estimated the annual production of the mines at more than 190 tons of gold and 635 tons of silver. By adding up the figures for Atahualpa's ransom and the loot taken at Cuzco, it has been calculated that the Spaniards obtained nearly 61,000 kilos of silver and 8,000 kilos of gold during the Conquest of Peru (Lothrop 1938). The melting down of the ransom alone kept nine furnaces burning for four months. The huge images of the sun and moon, the life-sized figures, the golden plates from the temple walls have disappeared for ever, and the loss to art and archaeology is incalcuable.

18. *Machu Picchu.*

BIBLIOGRAPHY

Alva, Walter (1988) *"Discovering the New World's Richest Unlooted Tomb"*. **National Geographic** 174 (4) 510 - 548.

- (1990) *"New Royal Tomb Unearthed"*. **National Geographic** 177 (6): 2 - 15.

Anton, F. (1987) **Ancient Peruvian Textiles.** London: Thames & Hudson.

Antze, Gustav (1965) **Trabajos en metal en el norte del Perú.** Lima: Universidad Nacional Mayor de San Marcos.

Baessler, Arthur (1906) **Altperuanische Metallgeräte.** Berlin.

Bennett, W. C. (1939) *"Archaeology of the North Coast of Peru"*. **Anthropological Papers.** American Museum of Natural History 37 (1): 1 - 153.

Beorchia Nigris, Antonio (1984) **El Enigma de los Santuarios Indígenas de Alta Montaña.** San Juan: Revista del Centro de Investigaciones de Alta Montaña. 5.

Bergsøe, Paul (1938) *"The gilding process and the metallurgy of copper and lead among the pre-Columbian Indians"*. **Ingeniorvidens kabelige Skrifter.** No. A46. Copenhagen: Naturvidenskabelige Samfund: Kommission hos, G.E.C. Gad.

Bird, Junius B. (1979) *"Legacy of the Stingless bee"*. **Natural History.** 88(9): 49 - 51.

Bray, Warwick (1972) *"Ancient American Metal-Smiths"*. **Proceedings of the Royal Anthropological Institute of Great Britain and Ireland for 1971:** 25 - 43. London.

- (1985) *"Ancient American Metallurgy: Five Hundred Years of Study"*. In Julie Jones (ed) **The Art of Pre-Columbian Gold: The Jan Mitchell Collection:** 76 - 84. London. Weidenfeld and Nicolson.

Brown, Dana (1984) **A Reconnaissance of Some Peruvian Goldworking Techniques.** Unpublished B.Sc. report. Institute of Archaeology, University College, London.

Bruhns, Karen Olsen (1976) *"The Moon Animal in northern Peruvian art and culture"*, **Ñawpa Pacha.** 14: 21 - 39.

Carcedo Muro, Paloma, and Izumi Shimada (1985) *"Behind the Golden Mask: Sicán Gold Artifacts from Batan Grande, Peru."* In Julie Jones (ed) **The Art of Pre-Columbian Gold: The Jan Mitchell Collection:** 61 - 75, London. Weidenfeld and Nicolson.

Carrión Cachot, R. (1948) *"La Cultura Chavín; dos nuevas colonias: Kunturwasi y Ancón."* **Revista del Museo Nacional.** 2(1): 123 - 172. Lima.

Chávez, Sergio Jorge (1987) *"Funerary offerings from a Middle Horizon context in Pomacanchi, Cuzco"*. **Ñawpa Pacha.** 22 - 23 (1984-5): 1-48.

de Lavalle, José Antonio and Werner Lang (eds) (1982) **Culturas Precolombinas: Chancay.** Lima: Banco de Crédito del Perú.

Disselhof, Hans-Dietrich (1971) **Vicús, eine Neu Entdeckte Altperuanische Kultur.** Berlin: Mann Verlag, Monumenta Americana 7.

- (1972) *"Metallschmuck aus der Loma Negra, Vicús (Nord-Peru)"*. **Antike Welt: Zeitschift für Archäologie und Urgeschichite** 3(2): 45 - 53.

Donnan, Christopher B, and Carol J. Mackey (1978) **Ancient Burial Patterns of the Moche Valley, Peru.** Austin and London: University of Texas Press.

Eisleb, Dieter and Renate Strelow (1980) **Altperuanische Kulturen III, Tiahuanaco.** Berlin: Museum für Völkerkunde, Veröffentlichungen des Museums für Völkerkunde, Berlin. N.F. 38, Abteilung Amerikanische Archäologie V.

Elera Arévalo, Carlos (1989) Untitled Report, **Willay** 32/33. 2 - 3.

Emmerich, André (1965) **Sweat of the Sun and Tears of the Moon: Gold and Silver in Pre-Columbian Art.** Seattle, University of Washington.

Epstein, Stephen M. and Izumi Shimada (1983) *"Metalúrgia de Sicán. Una reconstrucción de la producción de la aleación de cobre en el Cerro de los Cementerios, Perú"*. **Beiträge zur Allgemeinen und Vergleichenden Archäologie.** 5: 379 - 430.

Greider, Terence (1978) **The Art and Archaeology of Pashash.** Austin and London: University of Texas Press.

Grossman, Joel W. (1972) *"An Ancient Gold Worker's Tool Kit: The Earliest Metal Technology in Peru"*. **Archaeology.** 25(4): 270-275.

Helms, Mary W. (1981) *"Precious Metals and Politics; Style and Ideology in the Intermediate Area and Peru.* **Journal of Latin American Lore.** 7(2): 215 - 238.

Isbell, William H. (1984) *"Huari Urban Prehistory"*. In Ann Kendall (ed) **Current Archaeological Projects in the Central Andes: Some approaches and results:** 95 - 131 Oxford: British Archaeological Reports. International Series 210.

Jones, Julie (1979) *"Mochica Works of Art in Metal: A Review"*. In Elizabeth P. Benson (ed) **Pre-Columbian Metallurgy of South America:** 53 - 104. Washington D.C., Dumbarton Oaks Research Library and Collections.

Katz, Lois (ed) (1983) **Art of the Andes. Pre-Columbian Sculptures and Painted Ceramics from the Arthur M. Sackler Collections.** Washington D.C. The Arthur M. Sackler Foundation and the A.M.S. Foundation for the Arts, Sciences and Humanities.

Kaulicke, Peter (1988/9) Untitled report. **Willay** 29/30: 13 - 15.

Lechtman, Heather N. (1971) *"Ancient Methods of Gilding Silver: Examples from the Old and New Worlds."* In Robert H. Brill (ed) **Science and Archaeology:** 2-30. Cambridge: MIT Press.

- (1973) *"The Gilding of Metals in Pre-Columbian Peru."* In William J. Young (ed) **Application of Science in Examination of Works of Art.** 38 - 52. Boston, Museum of Fine Arts.

- (1977) *"Style in Technology - Some Early Thoughts."* In H. Lechtman and R. S. Merrill (eds) **Material Culture: Styles, Organization and Dynamics of Technology:** 3 - 20. 1975 Proceedings of the American Ethnological Society.

- (1979) *"Issues in Andean Metallurgy."* In E. P. Benson (ed) **Pre-Columbian Metallurgy of South America:** 1 - 40. Washington D. C., Dumbarton Oaks Research Library and Collection.

- (1981) *"Copper-Arsenic Bronzes from the North Coast of Peru."* In Anne-Marie Cantwell, James B. Griffin and Nan A. Rothschild (eds) **The Research Potential of Anthropological Museum Collections.** 77 - 121 New

York: Annals of the New York Academy of Sciences, Vol. 376.

- (1984A) *"Andean Value Systems and the Development of Prehistoric Metallurgy."* **Technology and Culture:** 25(1):1 - 36.

- (1984B) *"Pre-Columbian Surface Metallurgy."* **Scientific American.** 250(6): 56 - 63.

- (1988) *"Traditions and Styles in Central Andean Metallurgy."* In Robert Maddin (ed) **The Beginning of the Use of Metals and Alloys:** 344 - 378. Cambridge: MIT Press.

Lechtman, Heather, Antonieta Erlij, and Edward J. Barry Jr. (1982) *"New Perspectives in Moche Metallurgy: Techniques of Gilding Copper at Loma Negra. Northern Peru."* **American Antiquity** 47(1): 3 - 30.

Lothrop Samuel K. (1937) *"Gold and Silver from Southern Peru and Bolivia."* **Journal of the Royal Anthropological Institute.** LXVIII: 305 - 325. London.

- (1938) **Inca Treasure as Depicted by Spanish Historians.** Los Angeles Southwest Museum.

- (1941) *"Gold ornaments of the Chavin Style from Chongoyape, Peru."* **American Antiquity.** 6(3): 250 - 262.

- (1951) *"Gold Artifacts of the Chavin Style."* **American Antiquity** 16 (3): 226 - 240

Lumbreras, Luis Guillermo (1979) **El Arte y la Vida Vicus: Colección del Banco Popular.** Lima: Banco Popular.

Mathewson C.H. (1915) *"A metallographic description of some ancient bronzes from Machu Picchu,"* **American Journal of Science.** 40: 525 - 616.

McEwan, Colin, and María Isabel Silva (1989) *"¿Que fueron a hacer los Incas a la costa central del Ecuador?"* In J. F. Bouchard and M. Guinea (eds) **Relaciones interculturales an el area Ecuatorial del Pacífico durante la época Precolombina.** 163 - 185. Oxford: BAR International Series No. 503.

Menzel, Dorothy (1976) **Pottery Style and Society in Ancient Peru: Art as a Mirror of History in the Ica Valley, 1350 - 1570.** Berkeley: University of California Press.

- (1977) **The Archaeology of Peru and the Work of Max Uhle.** Berkeley : R. H. Lowie Museum of Anthropology, University of California.

Moseley, Michael E. (1978) **Peru's Golden Treasures.** Chicago. Field Museum of Natural History.

Mostny, Grete (ed) (1957) *"La Momia del Cerro El Plomo."* **Boletín del Museo Nacional de Historia Natural.** 27 (1). Santiago de Chile.

Onuki, Yoshio (1989) Untitled Report. **Willay.** 32/33: 11 - 15.

Paulsen, Allison Clement (1969) *"A Middle Horizon Tomb, Ica Valley, Peru.* **Ñawpa Pacha.** 6: 1 - 6.

Pimentel Gurmendi, Víctor (ed) (1981) **Tecnología de los Metales.** Lima: Museo Nacional de Antropología y Arqueología. Instituto Nacional de Cultura.

Proulx, Donald (1983) *"The Nasca Style."* In Lois Katz (ed) **Art of the Andes: Pre-Columbian Sculptured and Painted Ceramics from the Arthur M. Sackler Collections.** 87 - 105. Washington D. C. The Arthur M. Sackler Foundation and the AMS Foundation for the Arts, Sciences and Humanities.

Reichlin, Henrí (1941) *"Étude Technologique de Quelques Objects d'Or de Lambayeque, (Perú)."* **Journal de la Société des Américanistes,** Paris N.S. 33: 119 -154.

Ríos, Marcela and Enrique Retamozo (1978) *"Objetos de Metal Procedentes de la Isla de San Lorenzo."* **Arqueológicas.** 17. Lima.

Root, William C. (1949) *"Metallurgy."* In Julian H. Steward (ed) **Handbook of South American Indians.** 5: 205 - 225. Washington D. C. Smithsonian Institution. Bureau of American Ethnology.

Rowe, Ann Pollard (1984) **Costumes and Featherwork of the Lords of Chimor: Textiles from Peru's North Coast.** Washington D. C. The Textile Museum.

Rowe, John H. (1987) *"Machu Pijchu a la luz de los documentos del siglo XVI."* **Kuntur: Perú en la Cultura** 4 (marzo-abril). 12 - 20.

Rutledge, John W. and Robert B. Gordon (1987) *"The work of Metallurgical Artificers at Machu Picchu, Peru."* **American Antiquity** 52 (3): 578 - 594.

Sawyer, Alan R. (1968) **Mastercraftsmen of Ancient Peru.** New York: Solomon R. Guggenheim Foundation.

Schaffer, Anne-Louise (1981) **A Monster-Headed Complex of Mythical Creatures in Loma Negra Metalwork, M.S.** Paper presented at the 21st Anniversary Meeting of the Institute of Andean Studies: Berkeley, Jan 10 - 11, 1981.

- (1983) *"Cathartidae in Moche Art and Culture."* In J.F. Peterson (ed) **Flora and Flora Images in Pre-Columbian Cultures: Iconography and Function:** 29 - 68. Oxford: BAR International Series No. 171.

- (1986) *"Impressions in Metal: Reconstructing Burial context at Loma Negra, Peru,"* In Kvietok, D. Peter, and Daniel H. Sandweiss (eds) **Recent Studies in Andean Prehistory and Protohistory. Papers for the Second Annual Northeast Conference on Andean Archaeology and Ethnohistory:** 95 - 119. Cornell University, Latin American Studies Program.

Scott, David A. (1986) *"Fusion Gilding and Foil Gilding in Pre-Hispanic Colombia and Ecuador."* In C. Plazas (ed) **Metalúrgia de America Precolombina/Pre-Columbian American Metallurgy:** 310 - 325. Bogotá: Banco de la República.

Scott, David A. (1986) *"Gold and Silver Alloy Coatings over Copper. An Examination of Some Artefacts from Ecuador and Colombia."* **Archaeometry** 28, (1)., 33 - 50.

Shimada, Izumi (1987) *"Horizontal and vertical dimensions and prehistoric states in north Peru."* In Jonathan Haas, Shelia Pozorski, and Thomas Pozorski (eds) **The Origins and Development of the Andean State.** 130 - 144. Cambridge University Press.

- 1988/9) Untitled Report. **Willay.** 29/30: 15 -18.

Shimada, Izumi, Stephen Epstein, and Alan K. Craig (1982) *"Batan Grande: a Prehistoric Metallurgical Center in Peru."* **Science.** 216:952 - 959.

- (1983) *"The Metallurgical Process in Ancient North Peru."* **Archaeology.** 36(5): 38 - 45.

Tello, Julio C. and T Mejía Xesspe (1979) **Paracas, II Parte: Cavernas y Necrópolis.** Lima: Universidad Nacional Mayor de San Marcos/New York: Institute of Andean Research.

Tushingham, A.D., Ursula M Franklin, and Christopher Toogood (1979) **Studies in Ancient Peruvian Metalworking.** Royal Ontario Museum. History Technology and Art Monograph 3.

Von Schuler-Schömig, Immina (1972) **Werke Indianischer Goldschmiedekunst.** Berlin: Staatliche Museen Preussischer Kulturbesitz, Museen für Völkerkunde.

Wardwell, Allen (1968) **The Gold of Ancient America.** Greenwich; New York Graphic Society.

CATALOGUE

Sweat of the Sun

GOLD OF PERU · ORO DEL PERU

CATALOGUE ENTRIES

In attributing items in the exhibition to particular cultures we have adopted the ascriptions made by the lending institutions. We wish to emphasise that the use of the descriptions "gold" and "silver" in the catalogue is generic. As Dr. Bray points out in his article on pre-Hispanic Peruvian metalwork, many of the items manufactured by early Peruvian cultures were made of alloys rather than of pure gold and silver. Only metallurgical analysis could reveal the true make-up of many of the items in the exhibition but as yet this has not been much carried out. Consequently, exhibits have been categorised as "gold" or "silver" depending upon their surface appearance.

Each entry contains information given in the following order: catalogue number, title of object, brief description, cultural affiliation, dimensions (often including weight), name of lending institution, and museum registration number where known.

The undernoted abbreviations are used:

L – Length
W – Width
H – Height
D – Diameter
Wt. – Weight

§Chavín

1. GOLD EARSPOOL CENTREPIECE

Sheet gold centre decoration for an earspool, with a repoussé zoomorphic figure with feline attributes. Single perforation towards top edge.

CHAVIN

D: 9.7cm.
Wt: 21g.
Museo "Oro del Perú"
V-8/71.

2. GOLD EARSPOOL CENTREPIECE

Sheet gold centre decoration for an earspool, with a repoussé zoomorphic figure with feline attributes. Single perforation towards top.

CHAVIN

D. 9.7cm.
Wt: 21.5g.
Museo "Oro del Perú"
V-8/72.

3. PESTLE

Stone pestle with incised anthropomorphic double-sceptered figure with feline attributes.

CHAVIN

H: 6.5cm.
L: 19.5cm.
Museo "Oro del Perú"
V-3/19.

4. DISH (MORTAR)

Stone dish with incised feline, double-headed serpents and zoomorphic figures, contained between two bands.

CHAVIN

H: 9cm.
L: 24cm.
W: 15.5cm.
Museo "Oro del Perú"
V-3/20.

5. DISH

Stone dish with incised zoomorphic figures.

CHAVIN

D: 16cm.
Museo "Oro del Perú"
V-3/57.

6. MACE HEAD

Stone mace-head with incised zoomorphic figures of serpents with feline mouths on one side and on the other feline mouths.

CHAVIN

H: 4.4cm.
L: 13 cm.
W: 11.3 cm.
Museo "Oro del Perú"
V-3/250.

7. MACE HEAD

Stone mace-head with incised zoomorphic figures, featuring repeated eye design on one side and eye and feline mouth sequence on the other side.

CHAVIN

H: 4.4cm.
L: 13 cm.
W: 11.3cm
Museo "Oro del Perú"
V-3/248.

8. MACE HEAD

Stone mace-head, carved with zoomorphic figures.

CHAVIN

H: 11cm.
D: 10cm.
Museo "Oro del Perú"
V-6/68.

9. DISH

Stone dish, the base of which is incised with double-sceptered figures, with feline and reptilian attributes, contained within two circles. Round the border are feline creatures with chrysocolla inlay eyes. Ornamented inside the bowl with a zoomorphic figure with feline and reptilian attributes.

CHAVIN

H: 5cm.
D: 17 cm.
Museo "Oro del Perú"
M-3/446.

10. STIRRUP-SPOUT VESSEL

Ceramic vessel with lines and circles in high relief.

CHAVIN

H: 17cm.
W: 13.05cm.
Museo "Oro del Perú"
V-21A/19.

11. STIRRUP-SPOUT VESSEL

Burnished ceramic vessel with designs modelled in high relief representing zoomorphic and other figures.

CUPISNIQUE (Chavín)

H: 26cm.
W: 14cm.
Museo "Oro del Perú"
V-21A/07.

1   2

9

10

11

12

⬙ Cupisnique Chongoyape Vicús

12. CERAMIC VESSEL

Burnished grey pottery stirrup-spout vessel with a flat base and decoration of modelled stipples on the body. It has a thick, heavy stirrup spout with a plain upper section and a bevelled rim.

CUPISNIQUE

H: 19cm.
D: 16cm.
British Museum
1947 AM.10.1.

13. REPRESENTATION OF A FUNERAL IN GOLD AND COPPER

Two human figures carrying a mummy in a funerary litter, which is adorned with two miniature gold masks and a copper owl.

CHONGOYAPE

L: 18.2cm.
H: 7cm.
Wt: 298.05g.
Museo "Oro del Perú"
M-2/02.

14. NECKLACE

Necklace of alternate silver and rock crystal beads. The pendant is a polished opal sphere, held in place by a strip of copper. Restrung.

VICUS

L: 38cm.
Wt: 290g.
Museo "Oro del Perú"
V-5/56.

15. NECKLACE

Necklace of gold, rock crystal and red shell, with a pendant of the same materials but of larger dimensions. Restrung.

VICUS

L: 41 cm.
Museo "Oro del Perú"
V-3/21.

16. GOLD MASK

Round mask of repoussé sheet gold with lobulated ears. Disc-shaped pendants are suspended from the ears. The nose is perforated and the eyes are in high relief.

VICUS

H: 7.5cm.
D: 9.1cm.
Wt: 23.5g.
Museo "Oro del Perú"
V-15/444.

17. GILDED COPPER MASK

Mask of gilded copper with inlaid mother-of-pearl eyes and red shell inlay on the face. Traces of textile survive on reverse side. Perforations at either edge.

VICUS

H: 24.5cm.
W: 16cm.
Wt: 394.5g
Museo "Oro del Perú"
V-29/04.

18. GOLD PLATED COPPER MASK

Gold plated copper mask, representing an anthropomorphic face, with prominent eyebrows and open mouth. Inlaid with white and red shell.

VICUS

H: 9.7cm.
W: 10.5cm.
Wt: 64.5g.
Museo "Oro del Perú"
V-13/148.

19. SHEET OF GILDED COPPER

Sheet of openwork gilded copper with human face with attached headdress slotted on at the centre. The eyes and the mouth have mother-of-pearl inlays. There are zoomorphic figures on either side and six perforations.

VICUS

H: 20cm.
W: 24cm
Wt: 263g.
Museo "Oro del Perú"
V-48/22.

20. GOLD STRIPS

Long gold strips in the shape of feathers; the middle one is trapezoidal. There are 16 strips in all.

VICUS

H: 15.8cm.
W: 48.5cm.
Wt: 94g.
Museo "Oro del Perú"
V-13/36.

21. GOLD CONDOR HEAD

Sheet gold cut in the shape of a condor head; the crest, collar and beak are outlined.

VICUS

H: 7.4cm.
W: 8.3cm.
Wt: 13g.
Museo "Oro del Perú"
V-13/36.

△▽ *Vicús*

22. GOLD CROWN

Cylindrical sheet-gold crown, held in place by staples. The surface is covered with disc pendants which are attached to the crown by hooks (some missing). The top of the crown has ten double appendages, also with discs on hooks.

VICUS

H: 15cm.
D: 25.3cm.
Wt: 543g.
Museo "Oro del Perú"
V-17/20.

23. SILVER FOX HEAD

Oxidised silver fox head with eyes and teeth made of white shell and whiskers of wire. Discs are attached to the ears and jaws by hooks. The pieces of which it is made up are joined by stapling and slotting with tabs.

VICUS

H: 9cm.
W: 14cm.
Wt: 279g.
Museo "Oro del Perú"
V-48/102.

24. GOLD AND SILVER NOSE ORNAMENT

Nose ornament made of a sheet of gold joined to one of silver. Semi-circular in shape, the upper edge is straight and has an oval aperture. The decoration consists of two felines, their bodies seen in profile, and faces in full. The perimeter is outlined with repoussé dots.

VICUS

H: 8.7cm.
W: 11.2cm.
Wt: 15.5g.
Museo "Oro del Perú"
V-41/77.

25. GOLD AND SILVER NOSE ORNAMENT

Nose ornament of gold and silver made of two pieces joined together. Semi-circular in shape, the upper edge is straight with a round aperture. It is decorated with two circular human faces. The perimeter is outlined with repoussé dots.

VICUS

H: 12.8cm.
W: 16.2cm.
Wt: 97.5g.
Museo "Oro del Perú"
V-41/118.

26. GOLD AND SILVER NOSE ORNAMENT

Rectangular nose ornament of sheet gold and silver. The gold border includes gold appendages which emerge from the top and terminate in figures of parrots. The sides are hung with green beads attached with hooks; at the top edge there is a circular aperture. The central sheet of silver has a standing human figure with outstretched arms and serpents hanging from the waist. It has a moveable head attached with hooks, a face in relief and a headdress with two pendants. There are traces of red paint.

VICUS

H: 11cm.
W: 19cm.
Wt: 33g.
Museo "Oro del Perú"
V-41/115.

27. GOLD AND SILVER NOSE ORNAMENT

Nose ornament of ovoid gold sheets. The top part has a round aperture. It is decorated with a repoussé anthropomorphic head of burnt silver, which is attached by two tabs that slot into the back plate. Traces of red paint on the back.

VICUS

H: 4.7cm
W: 6.9cm.
Wt: 12.5g.
Museo "Oro del Perú"
V-42/17.

28. GOLD AND COPPER NOSE ORNAMENT

Nose ornament made of two sheets joined together, one of gold and the other of copper. The lower part is semi-circular, the two upper ends curve outwards, and there is a circular aperture in the centre. Repoussé dots outline the perimeter of each sheet.

VICUS

H: 21cm.
W: 26cm.
Wt: 120.5g.
Museo "Oro del Perú"
V-19/26.

△̇⊙̇△̇ Vicús   Recuay   Paracas

29. COPPER FIGURE

Figure of a musician, who stands with his hands towards his mouth, one of which holds a trumpet. He wears hanging spiral earrings and a necklace of semi-spherical pendants. The figure has a semi-circular cape-like sheet on its back, and a waistband with pendants. Also inlaid eyes of mother-of-pearl.

VICUS

H: 22.3cm.
W: 11.5cm.
Wt: 350g.
Museo "Oro del Perú"
V-1/041.

30. GOLD RATTLE

Gold rattle in the shape of an axe, surmounted by representations of gourds, which contain small balls of copper. A horizontal tube is attached to a strip linking the gourds. The blade is incomplete. Made from one sheet of embossed metal doubled over. It retains traces of red paint.

VICUS

H: 32.5cm.
W: 23.6cm.
Wt: 822.5g. (with acrylic support)
Museo "Oro del Perú"
V-8/02.

31. CERAMIC VESSEL

Ceramic bridge-handled whistling vessel. The lentoid body and upward facing head, which has modelled and perforated eyes and a nose, are decorated with resist designs in chestnut, white and sepia. At the base of the neck, and on the body, is a small flange.

VICUS

H: 21cm.
L: 18cm.
W: 16.3cm.
British Museum
1967 AM.8.5.

32. GOLD ORNAMENT

Sheet-gold jaguar-head mask with a suggestion of eyes (2 holes), a nose in relief and a fanged open-cut mouth. It is damaged and around the edges are paired holes with staples.

VICUS (Piura)

H: 11.2cm.
W: 9.7cm.
Wt: 41.17g.
British Museum
1966 AM.6.5.

33. GOLD PLATED ORNAMENT

Large sheet-gold crescentic ear ornament with centre cut out. This is circular and around it there is a stepped fret pattern, possibly in silver.

VICUS (Piura)

H: 8.8cm.
L: 7.3cm.
W: 8.9cm.
Wt: 44.5g.
British Museum
1966 AM. 6.1.

34. GOLD ORNAMENT

Gold semi-circular ornament (possibly a nose ornament), with a concave side.

VICUS

H: 5cm.
W: 5.7cm.
Wt: 17.35g.
British Museum
1966 AM.6.2.

35. GOLD AND COPPER SERPENT

Gold and copper alloy repoussé serpent with an open work nose, mouth and additional incised ornamentation with 8 perforations.

VICUS (Piura)

L: 23cm.
W: 6cm.
Wt: 38.81g.
British Museum
1966 AM.6.6.

36. CERAMIC VESSEL

Bridge-handled vessel with spout depicting a head on a round body. The figure and two dragonlike creatures are depicted in black and white on chestnut.

RECUAY

H: 13.50cm.
D: 12cm.
British Museum
1909-4-3.1.

37. HUMAN SKULL

Human skull with a double trepanation. The front cavity is covered by a sheet of gold. The back cavity, which is smaller, is not covered.

PARACAS

Museo "Oro del Perú"
V-37/05.

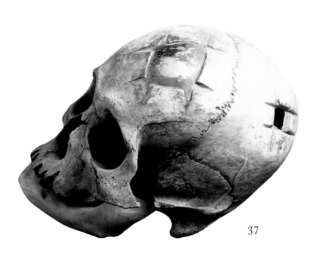

37

19

21

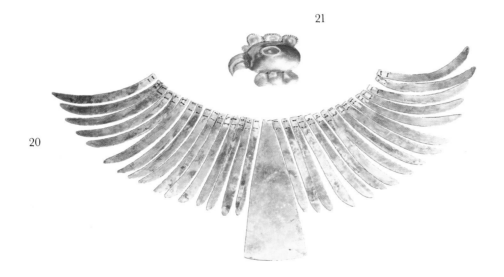

20

31

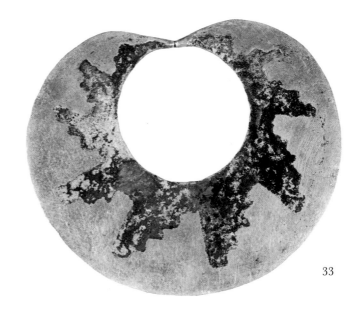

33

17

38

34

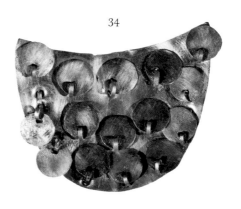

30

34

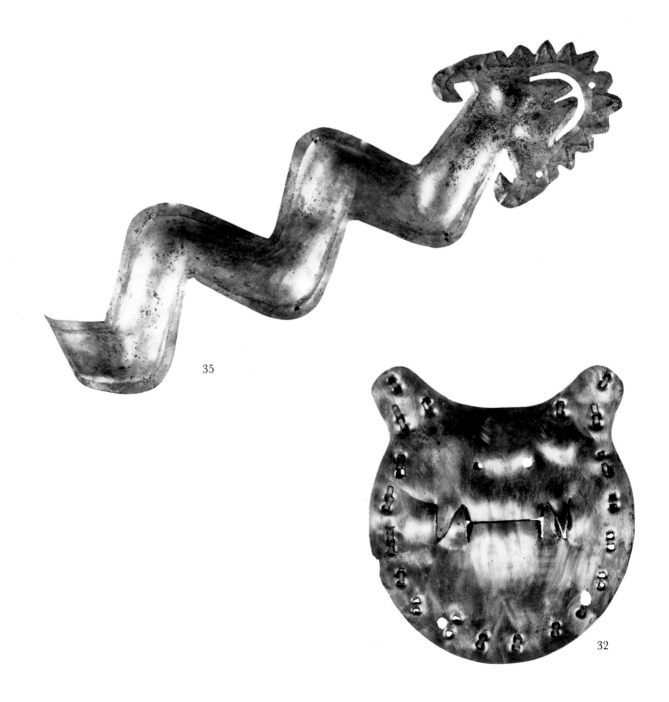

35

32

41

49

51

38. GOLD BOWL

Gold bowl with converging undulating sides and a convex base.

MOCHE

H: 8cm.
D: 13.1cm.
Wt: 107g.
Museo "Oro del Perú"
V-71/09.

39. GOLD CUP

Gold cup with curved sides. Small, slightly concave, base and converging rim.

MOCHE

H: 7.5cm.
D: 13.3cm.
Wt: 150.5g.
Museo "Oro del Perú"
V-72/13.

40. GOLD BOWL

Gold bowl with slightly converging sides and convex base.

MOCHE

H: 4.5cm.
D: 12.2cm.
Wt: 106.5g.
Museo "Oro del Perú"
V-72/17.

41. GOLD CUP

Gold cup modelled in the shape of a human head. Flat base. The lower part of the sides converge slightly and the central part has a face in relief. The nose has a nose-ring and the ears are attached by staples. The upper part is of a headdress with repoussé geometric designs. Manufactured from several sheets of gold.

MOCHE

H: 17cm.
W: 9 cm.
Wt: 136g.
Museo "Oro del Perú"
V-76/38.

42. GOLD CONTAINER

Concave gold container, decorated with small hooks and circular pendants.

MOCHE

H: 7.0cm.
D: 10.5cm.
Wt: 189g.
Museo "Oro del Perú"
V-71/16.

43. LARGE GOLD CUP

Gold cup with a conical foot.

MOCHE

H: 10.2cm.
D: 13.1cm.
Wt: 201.5g.
Museo "Oro del Perú"
V-72/08.

44. LARGE GOLD CUP

Gold cup with a conical foot

MOCHE

H: 9.8cm.
D: 12.8cm.
Wt: 205g.
Museo "Oro del Perú"
V-72/10.

45. GOLD SPOON

Gold spoon with a handle in the shape of an undulating serpent.

MOCHE

L: 18.5cm.
W: 2cm.
Wt: 12.5g.
Museo "Oro del Perú"
V-87/71.

46. GOLD SPOON

Gold spoon with cast finial in the form of a deer and two birds.

MOCHE

L: 7.7cm.
W: 2.1cm.
Wt: 15g.
Museo "Oro del Perú"
V-87/87.

47. GOLD SPOON

Gold spoon with finial in the form of two decorative spirals.

MOCHE

L: 8.2cm.
W: 2cm.
Wt: 7g.
Museo "Oro del Perú"
V-87/89.

₰Moche

48. GOLD LADLE

Undecorated gold ladle.

MOCHE

L: 33.5cm.
D: 11.3cm.
Wt: 224g.
Museo "Oro del Perú"
V-71/23.

49. INLAID GOURD

Gourd with mother-of-pearl and shell inlays,
forming a row of anthropomorphic figures with
faces in high relief and wearing semi-circular
headdresses. The base has a circle enclosing disc-
shaped inlays.

MOCHE

H: 8.5cm.
D: 20cm.
Museo "Oro del Perú"
V-62/63.

50. GOLD CHISEL

Solid gold chisel, trapezoidal in shape. The cutting
edge is semi-circular.

MOCHE

H: 14.3cm.
W: 3cm.
Wt: 16.5g.
Museo "Oro del Perú"
V-16/88.

51. GOLD EARRING

Gold earring in the shape of an owl, with turquoise
inlay. It hangs from a ring of plaited gold thread.

MOCHE

H: 7.2cm.
W: 4cm.
Wt: 20g.
Museo "Oro del Perú"
V-19/48.

52. GOLD EARRING

Gold earring with four pendants of rock crystal.
Gold ring.

MOCHE

H: 9.3cm.
W: 4.6cm.
Wt: 39g.
Museo "Oro del Perú"
V-19/55.

53-54. GOLD EARRINGS

Pair of tubular gold earrings, with central
decorations of gold threads and small spheres.

MOCHE

53. H: 5.5cm.	54. H: 5.7cm.
W: 2.8cm.	W: 2.9cm.
Wt: 18g.	Wt: 19g.

Museo "Oro del Perú"
V-19/97-98.

55-56. GOLD ORNAMENTS

Pair of bird-shaped ornaments made of sheet gold
and wire. Both have a head, wings, crest, beak,
limbs and a gold ring on the back attached by wire.
One retains a gold disc hanging from its beak and
turquoise inlay eyes.

MOCHE

55. H: 8cm.	H: 7.8cm.
W: 6cm.	W: 6cm.
Wt: 23g.	Wt: 23g.

Museo "Oro del Perú"
V-19/49-50.

57-58. GOLD ORNAMENTS

Pair of gold ornaments with bird bodies and human
faces, decorated with small spheres and pendants.
Both have rings on the back and one retains legs.

MOCHE

57. L: 4.2cm.	58. L: 4.1cm.
W: 2.6cm.	W: 2.6cm.
Wt: 14g.	Wt: 14.5g.

Museo "Oro del Perú"
V-19/93-94.

59-60. EARSPOOLS

Pair of gold earspools, disc-shaped, with settings of
stones, shell and strips of gold, at the centre of which
are figures with zoomorphic features. Surrounded
by gold spheres. Mounted on tubes at right angles to
the convex bases.

MOCHE

59. H: 10.6cm.	60. H: 10.2cm.
D: 6.4cm.	D: 6.5cm.
Wt: 120.5g	Wt: 120.5g.

Museo "Oro del Perú"
V-10/98-99.

61-62. GOLD EARSPOOLS

Pair of earspools, disc-shaped, with mosaics of semi-precious stones (lapis lazuli, chrysocolla, turquoise) and shell of different colours representing anthropomorphic figures with avian features. Surrounded by gold spheres. Mounted on large tubes which taper slightly towards the base.

MOCHE

61. H: 5.8cm.   62. H: 5.1cm.
     D: 11.4cm.   D: 11.7cm.
     Wt: 162g.   Wt: 162.5g.
Museo "Oro del Perú"
V-12/107-108.

63-64. SILVER EARSPOOLS

Pair of silver earspools encircled by filigree and adorned with human heads in chrysocolla, lapis lazuli and red shell. At the centres are human figures worked in gold. Some of the small spheres round the edges of the discs are missing. Mounted on tubes decorated with geometrical motifs. The bases are ornamented with repoussé animals.

MOCHE

63. H: 5.2cm.   64. H: 5.2cm.
     W: 8.7cm.   D: 9cm.
     Wt: 82g.   Wt: 87g.
Museo "Oro del Perú"
M1/17-18.

65-66. GOLD EARSPOOLS

Pair of disc-shaped earspools. Filigree decoration encircles figures of warriors surrounded by attached discs. Cylindrical tubes.

MOCHE

65. D: 12cm.   66. D: 12cm.
     L: 5.4cm   L: 5.4cm.
     Wt: 125.5g   Wt: 123.5g
Museo "Oro del Perú"
M-1/34-34.

67. GOLD TWEEZERS

Lunate gold tweezers. The two extremities are ornamented with zoomorphic heads with curved crests and gold cords around the eyes and mouth. Small discs are suspended from the eyes. In the upper centre is a monkey-like creature.

MOCHE

H: 10.7cm.
W: 11.4cm.
Wt: 63g.
Museo "Oro del Perú"
V-16/17.

68. GOLD TWEEZERS

Semi-circular gold tweezers, with a ring-shaped handle on the upper section.

MOCHE

H: 13.4cm.
W: 16.8cm.
Wt: 48.5g.
Museo "Oro del Perú"
V-16/21.

§Moche

69. GOLD TWEEZERS

Gold tweezers in the form of a double-headed serpent. On top is a human face surrounded by double-headed serpent motifs, attached to which is a tubular loop.

MOCHE

H: 6.7cm.
W: 5cm.
Wt: 10g.
Museo "Oro del Perú"
V-19/255.

70. GOLD TWEEZERS

Gold tweezers in the form of a double-headed serpent. On top is a human face, with pendants hanging from the ears, and a double-headed serpent. A tubular loop provides suspension.

MOCHE

H: 5cm.
W: 7.3cm.
Wt: 14.5g.
Museo "Oro del Perú"
V-19/298.

71. GOLD TWEEZERS

Gold tweezers in the form of a double-headed serpent. On top is a human figure with a ring attached to its head.

MOCHE

H: 18cm.
W: 12.7cm.
Wt: 61.5g.
Museo "Oro del Perú"
V-17A/11.

72. GOLD TWEEZERS

Circular gold tweezers with a ring in the centre.

MOCHE

H: 7.8cm.
W: 7cm.
Wt: 61g.
Museo "Oro del Perú"
V-19/245.

73. SMALL GOLD MASK

Gold mask with turquoise earspools, a mother-of-pearl nose ornament and silver eyes.

MOCHE

H: 13.1cm.
W: 13.6cm.
Wt: 36.5g.
Museo "Oro del Perú"
V-26/08.

𝕄oche

74. SMALL GOLD MASK

Small gold mask, with a silver headdress from the front of which hang two disc-shaped pendants. It has turquoise earspools.

MOCHE

H: 14cm.
W: 12cm.
Wt: 42g.
Museo "Oro del Perú"
V-26/06.

75. GOLD AND SILVER HEAD

Small human head of gold and silver. Four perforations on back of head.

MOCHE

H: 6cm.
W: 5.2cm.
Wt: 34g.
Museo "Oro del Perú"
V-87/185.

76. GOLD SPEAR THROWER

Tapering sheet-gold spear thrower with a hook at one end. Decorated at the opposite end with a small bird.

MOCHE

L: 30.5cm.
W: 3.8cm.
Wt: 61g.
Museo "Oro del Perú"
V-11/27.

77. PAN PIPES

Panpipes comprising 9 copper tubes closed at the ends. Held together by a gold band ornamented with repoussé human figures.

MOCHE

H: 15.5cm.
W: 11.2cm.
Museo "Oro del Perú"
M-1/142.

78. GOLD IDOL

Gold idol, wearing a headdress and poncho, sitting on a serpent's or lizard's head. Details picked out in gold wire.

MOCHE (from Frias or possibly Ecuador)

H: 8.5cm.
W: 2.5cm.
Wt: 33.5g.
Museo "Oro del Perú"
V-16/41.

79. GOLD IDOL

Gold idol with raised arms, silver belt, chrysocolla eyes and pendants hanging from its head. It has two flanges with perforations on the back.

MOCHE

H: 6.5cm.
W: 5cm.
Wt: 22.5g.
Museo "Oro del Perú"
V-16/130.

80. GOLD IDOL

Gold idol with raised arms. Clothing has a zig-zag decoration.

MOCHE

H: 8cm.
W: 3.7cm.
Wt: 14.5g.
Museo "Oro del Perú"
V-16/131.

81. GOLD IDOL

Gold idol with raised arms. Made of several sheets of gold joined together. The face is decorated with gold thread and has a headdress to which four round pendants are attached with hooks. It has appliqué eyes, nose and mouth. There are two sets of perforations on the back.

MOCHE

H: 12.5cm.
W: 5.8cm.
Wt: 69.5g.
Museo "Oro del Perú"
V-16/125.

82. GOLD IDOL

Gold idol with raised arms. Made of several sheets of gold joined together. The figure is hollow and the face is decorated with soldered gold thread around the rim. Pendants hang from the ears.

MOCHE

H: 9cm.
W: 3.6cm.
Wt: 23.5g.
Museo "Oro del Perú"
V-16/120.

§Moche

83-84. GOLD GLOVES

Pair of sheet-gold gloves (for right and left hands). The fingers are outstretched and there are slots which may once have held applied silver nails. The inner side of the left hand glove is "sewn" along the seam with a strip of gold.

MOCHE

83. (Right hand)   84. (Left hand)
H: 22.5cm.   H: 20.5cm.
W: 12cm.   W: 10.8cm.
Museo "Oro del Perú"
V-25/02-03.

85. GOLD BAG

Sheet-gold bag in the shape of an animal with applied and soldered eyes, snout, genitals, tail and limbs. The head and snout have hooks from which round and triangular pendants are suspended. On the back it is decorated with repoussé geometrical designs, crosses, saltires and zigzag patterns, framed within panels.

MOCHE

H: 38cm.
W: 16cm.
Wt: 328g.
Museo "Oro del Perú"
V-26/02.

86. GOLD PECTORAL

Crescent-shaped gold pectoral, with an applied jaguar head in the middle.

MOCHE

H: 18cm.
W: 25cm.
Wt: 121.5g.
Museo "Oro del Perú"
V-26/04.

87. GOLD BELT

Gold belt, with an applied feline head in relief which has an openwork mouth at the centre. The whiskers are made of gold threads and the tongue is made of a triangular pendant. Disc-shaped pendants hang from the ears.

MOCHE

W: 20.5cm.
L: 57.5cm.
Wt: 166.5g.
Museo "Oro del Perú"
V-26/07.

88. GOLD HEAD

Zoomorphic head with sheet-gold ears. The eyes and mouth are formed by gold threads and at either side there are hooks from which round pendants hang. It has a sheet of gold representing the teeth of the lower jaw. The figure has a socketed neck, which would have been slotted into another object.

MOCHE

W: 4.5cm.
L: 4.4cm.
Wt: 13.5g.
Museo "Oro del Perú"
V-19/102.

89. ZOOMORPHIC GOLD LIZARD

Lizard of sheet gold with turquoise eyes and four triangular pendants attached to the top. The belly has two soldered sheets with crossed hooks, which have pendants at both ends.

MOCHE

L: 39.8cm.
Wt: 66g.
Museo "Oro del Perú"
V-19/313.

90. GOLD CONE

Conical object of alternate white and yellow gold strips. It has a large perforation close to the rim and two small ones near the top.

MOCHE

H: 7.6cm.
D: 5.7cm.
Wt: 39.5g.
Museo "Oro del Perú"
V-19/74.

91. GOLD HEAD DEFORMER

Sheet-gold strip which may have been used as a head deformer. One end is rounded and the other angled. Single perforations at both ends.

MOCHE

W: 2.4cm.
L: 114cm.
Wt: 50.5g.
Museo "Oro del Perú"
V-16/53

74

89

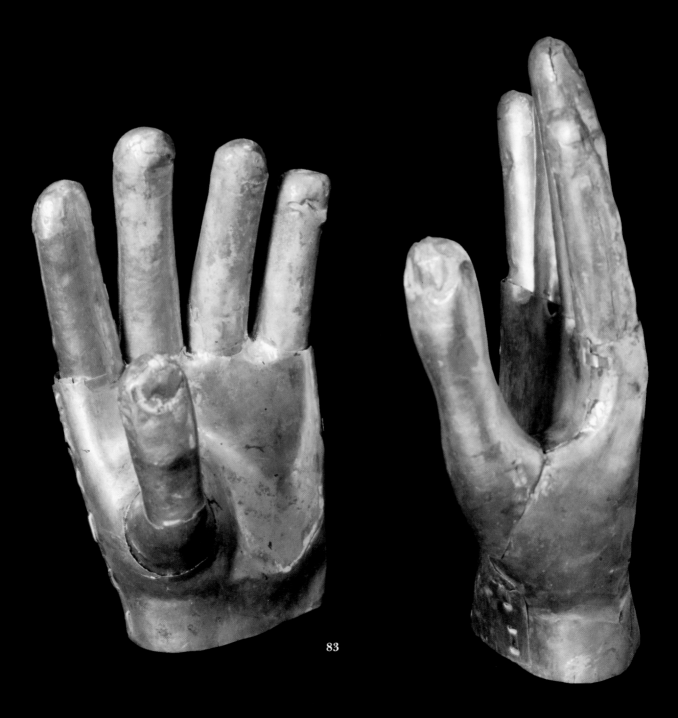

83

84

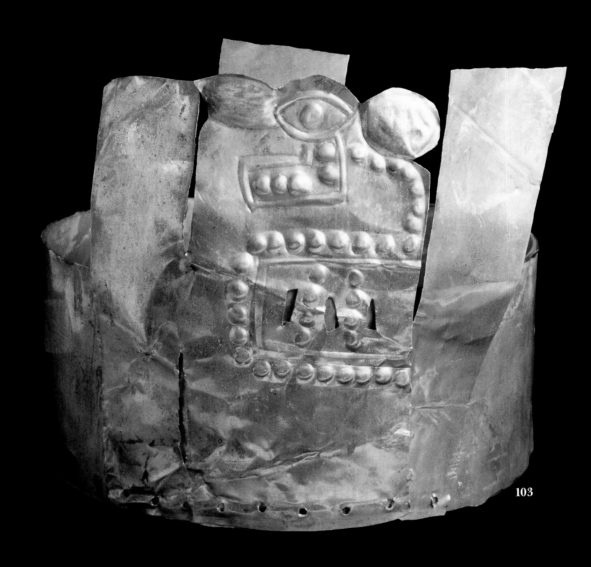

103

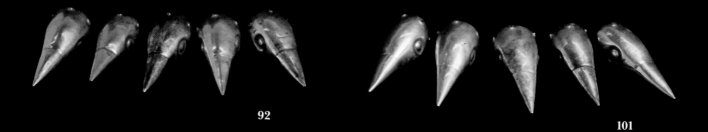

92

101

107

105

43

36

92-101. GOLD FINGER TIPS

Gold finger tips in the shape of birds' heads. Each example has five perforations around the edge.

MOCHE

92.	H: 4.5cm. D: 1.6cm. Wt: 6.5g.	93.	H: 4.5cm. D: 1.8cm. Wt: 6.5g
94.	H: 4.5cm. D: 1.8cm. Wt: 6.5g.	95.	H: 4.7cm. D: 1.9cm. Wt: 6.5g.
96.	H. 4.6cm. D: 1.8cm. Wt: 6.5g.	97.	H: 4.5cm. D: 2cm. Wt: 6.5g.
98.	H: 4.8cm. D: 1.8cm. Wt: 7.5g.	99.	H: 4.7cm. D: 1.8cm. Wt: 7g.
100.	H: 4.7cm. D: 1.8cm. Wt: 6.5g.	101.	H: 4.6cm. D: 1.6cm. Wt: 6g.

Museo "Oro del Perú"
V-13/122-131.

102. GOLD CROWN

Sheet-gold crown with trapezoidal crenellations around the upper rim. The lower part has perforations and embossed points arranged in parallel lines. The strip is linked at the ends by a staple.

MOCHE

H: 5.5cm.
W: 18cm.
Wt: 156g.
Museo "Oro del Perú"
V-18/12.

103. GOLD CROWN

Sheet-gold crown with projecting rectangular panels and a zoomorphic figure outlined with repoussé dots and lines.

MOCHE

H: 14.1cm.
W: 15.6cm.
Wt: 123g.
Museo "Oro del Perú"
V-19/08.

104. GOLD DIADEM

Gold diadem comprising a band of sheet gold, ornamented along its lower edge by seven attached birds. They have turquoise bead eyes and spangles suspended from their beaks. The central bird is larger than the others and one now lacks its head. A fan-shaped plume with embossed points at the front of the diadem may not be original to the piece.

MOCHE (Frías)
D: 18.8cm.
H: 4.8cm. (without plume)
   17.0cm. (with plume)
Wt: 137g. (including acrylic support)
Museo "Oro del Perú"
V-24/35.

Moche

105. NECKLACE

Necklace consisting of four strands of oval and round gold beads. At the top there is a figure carved in chrysocolla, and on either side tubes and beads of the same material. Restrung.

MOCHE

L: 29.5cm.
Museo "Oro del Perú"
V-5/52.

106. NECKLACE

Gold necklace with pendants in the shape of a variety of small masks, serpents and cones. At the bottom is a long snake-like pendant with eyes made of red shell. Restrung.

MOCHE

L: 62cm.
Wt: 147g.
Museo "Oro del Perú"
V-40/01.

107. COLLAR

Gold collar consisting of three strands of spherical beads, separated by oval beads. It also has pendants comprising both types of beads. Restrung.

MOCHE

L: 49cm.
W: 8.5cm.
Wt: 144.5g.
Museo "Oro del Perú"
V-39/01.

108-109. GOLD BREAST ORNAMENTS

Pair of gold breast ornaments. Discs with trapezoidal pendants adorned by spangles, from which hang serpent-shaped strips. The discs are ornamented by gold spheres around the edges, birds and red shell discs at the centre, which bear a further bird.

MOCHE

108.	L: 18cm. D of disc: 7cm. Wt: 45g.	109.	L: 18cm. D of disc: 7cm. Wt: 46g.

Museo "Oro del Perú"
V-8/33-35

110-111. GOLD BREAST ORNAMENTS

Pair of gold breast ornaments. Discs with trapezoidal pendants, from which hang serpent-shaped strips, each supporting a semicircular spangle. The discs are ornamented with gold spheres around the edges and are richly decorated with attached small discs and spangles. At the centre is a bird with inlaid turquoise eyes.

MOCHE

110. L: 29cm.   *111.* L: 29cm.
     D of disc: 10cm.   D of disc: 10cm.
     Wt: 115g   Wt: 115g
Museo "Oro del Perú"
V-11/10-11.

112. SEA SHELL WITH INCISED AND INLAID DESIGNS

Sea shell with superimposed human head. Inlays of chrysocolla, brown stone and coloured shell represent a human body and zoomorphic and other motifs.

MOCHE (Frías)

L: 12.02cm.
W: 10cm.
Museo "Oro del Perú"
V-54/72.

113. SEA SHELL WITH INCISED AND INLAID DESIGNS

Sea shell, with inlays of shells of different colours and mother-of-pearl representing a human face and zoomorphic figure.

MOCHE

L: 10.02cm.
W: 11cm.
Museo "Oro del Perú"
V-54/70.

114. COTTON PONCHO

Black cotton poncho, dyed, with gilded silver decorations representing double-sceptered figures.

MOCHE

L: 85cm.
W: 77cm.
Museo "Oro del Perú"

115. WOODEN SCEPTRE

Carved wooden sceptre surmounted by a seated figure under an awning. The figure has one inlaid eye, wears a cap and has large earlobes. The right hand holds what is possibly a cup. The awning retains traces of paint. The shaft of the sceptre is cylindrical with, at the top, five carved heads which probably once had inlaid eyes. The back of the upper section is flat and has a central ridge with two windows on either side. It retains traces of dark red and white paint.

MOCHE? (Macabi Island)

H: 57cm.
W: 11cm.
British Museum
7433.

Moche

116. PORTRAIT VESSEL

Portrait-head vessel (without stirrup) in ochre, cream and chestnut, with circular geometrical designs in sepia. It has a flat base.

MOCHE

H: 21cm.
W: 19.30cm.
D: 14cm.
D rim: 9.2cm.
British Museum
c.c.1939.

117. CERAMIC VESSEL

Stirrup-spout vessel modelled in the shape of a condor or turkey-buzzard (gallinazo). With incised and painted decoration in cream and chestnut paint or slips.

MOCHE (Phase I)

H: 21cm.
D: 16cm.
W: 11cm.
British Museum
1947. AM.10.3.

118. CERAMIC VESSEL

Stirrup-spout vessel with globular body. Ornamented with scenes depicting fish, reeds, nets and birds (egrets?) in chestnut-red paint on a cream background. The body is surmounted by a duck (possibly a torrent duck), modelled with incised details and painted with chestnut-red highlights.

MOCHE (PHASE IV, Chicama Valley)

H: 23.5cm.
D: 10.5cm.
British Museum
1909. 12-18.75

119. CERAMIC VESSEL

Stirrup-spout vessel with body in the shape of a house or temple. The body is surmounted by an awning covering four figures, possibly musicians (two figures may be missing). Around the base are running figures painted in chestnut-red on a red base.

MOCHE (PHASE IV, Chicama Valley)

H: 19cm.
W: 12cm.
British Museum
1909. 12-18.77

120. CERAMIC VESSEL

Stirrup-spout vessel with painted scene on body in chestnut-red on a cream base depicting a mythological fishing scene. The stirrup is painted and the vessel has a flat base.

MOCHE (PHASE IV)

H: 29.5cm.
D base: 12cm.
British Museum
1909.12-18.119.

121. GOLD PENANNULAR NOSE (OR EAR) ORNAMENT

Crescentic sheet-gold ornament with embossed points. Within the inner ring there are 8 open-work spirals running in one direction. Some reddish discolouration.

MOCHE (Pacasmayo)

H: 3.9cm.
D: 4.1cm.
Wt: 4.55g.
British Museum
1907.3-19.392.

122. GOLD VESSEL

Gold cup representing a human head modelled in relief. The back of the head bears decorations in the form of ears of maize. The upper part of the vessel is stepped, ending in a flaring mouth.

NAZCA

H: 23.2cm.
D: 11.5cm.
Wt: 193g.
Museo "Oro del Perú"
V-71/11.

123. GOLD VESSEL

Gold cup representing a human head with features modelled in relief. There are remains of paint round the eyes and mouth. The back of the head bears decorations in the shape of ears of maize. The upper part of the vessel is stepped ending in a flaring mouth. It has incised saltires at the rim.

NAZCA

H: 24.6cm.
D: 9.2cm.
Wt: 95.5g.
Museo "Oro del Perú"
V-70/19.

124. GOLD VESSEL

Gold cup representing a human head with features modelled in relief. The back of the head bears decorations in the shape of ears of maize. Traces of red paint remain on the face. The upper portion has straight walls, is decorated with embossed roundels and ends in a flaring mouth.

NAZCA

H: 16.3cm.
D: 7.3cm.
Wt: 116g.
Museo "Oro del Perú"
V-78/18.

Nazca

125. SILVER VESSEL

Silver cup representing a head with features modelled in relief. The back of the head bears decorations in the shape of ears of maize. The upper portion is decorated with embossed roundels near the face (perhaps representing a headdress) and ends in a flaring mouth.

NAZCA

H: 27.5cm.
D: 14.2cm.
Wt: 342g.
Museo "Oro del Perú"
V-68/13.

126. GOLD AND SILVER VESSEL

Cup of alternate gold and silver sections with, at the centre, a human face modelled in relief. The top of the vessel has a flaring bevelled rim.

NAZCA

H: 22.5cm.
D: 10.5cm
Wt: 230.5g.
Museo "Oro del Perú"
V-82/20.

127. GOLD MASK

Sheet-gold mask in the shape of a stylised human face ornamented with repoussé broken lines and bosses. By way of hair, there are three groups of five strips ending in serpent's heads. There are four perforations around the nose.

NAZCA

H: 19.7cm.
W: 21.8cm.
Wt: 81g.
Museo "Oro del Perú"
V-07/08.

128. GOLD MASK

Sheet-gold mask in the shape of a stylised human face. Hair is represented by strips ending in serpent's heads. It has four groups of two perforations.

NAZCA

H: 14.3cm.
W: 17.5cm.
Wt: 31.5g.
Museo "Oro del Perú"
V-14/04.

129. GOLD BRACELET

Gold bracelet with repoussé circles at either end. The central section is undecorated. There are two perforations on either edge.

NAZCA

L: 8.7cm.
W: 19.7cm.
Wt: 30g.
Museo "Oro del Perú"
V-35/26.

130. GOLD BRACELET

Gold bracelet made of a single rectangular sheet with rounded ends. It is decorated with repoussé dots, broken lines and concentric circles. It has one perforation at either edge.

NAZCA

L: 17cm.
W: 7.7cm.
Wt: 18g.
Museo "Oro del Perú"
V-35/19.

131. GOLD WRISTBAND

Sheet-gold wristband of trapezoidal shape with rounded ends. It is decorated with repousse circular and linear designs. It has one perforation at either edge.

NAZCA

L: 12.5cm.
W: 16cm.
Wt: 195g.
Museo "Oro del Perú"
V-35/08.

132. GOLD LEGBAND

Gold legband ornamented with rows of quatrefoil bosses.

NAZCA

L: 25cm.
W: 20.1cm.
Wt: 205.5g.
Museo "Oro del Perú"
V-35/66.

133. GOLD SPATULA

Gold spatula, ornamented with cast parrot finial.

NAZCA

H: 6.7cm.
W: 2cm.
Wt: 9g.
Museo "Oro del Perú"
V-15/64.

134. GOLD SPATULA

Gold spatula ornamented with a cast finial in the form of a bird eating an ear of maize.

NAZCA

H: 8.1cm.
W: 2.2cm.
Wt: 9.5g.
Museo "Oro del Perú"
V-15/25.

135. GOLD SPATULA

Cast gold spatula with a hummingbird modelled on the upper part.

NAZCA

H: 7.7cm.
W: 3.2cm.
Wt: 8g.
Museo "Oro del Perú"
V-15/38.

136. HELMET

Helmet made of vegetable fibres, tied and bound together by thick cotton thread. The surface fibres have been wrapped with small tubular strips of gold foil.

NAZCA

H: 20cm.
D: 28.5cm.
Wt: 573g.
Museo "Oro del Perú"
V-61/13.

137. GOLD AND SILVER SCALES

Gold and silver open-work scales on a rectangular silver balancing beam, in which six little birds are enclosed, facing inwards - three on either side. The top of the beam has a stepped fret design. The two small bowls are attached by cords to gold balls which support them; a third cord at the centre maintains the balance point for suspension.

NAZCA

L. of beam: 10.2cm.
W. of beam: 3cm.
D. of bowls: 5.9cm.
Wt: 95.5g.
Museo "Oro del Perú"
V-35/60.

138. ANDEAN FLUTE (QUENA)

Reed pipe with five applied gold rings.

NAZCA

L: 35.5cm.
D: 2cm.
Museo "Oro del Perú"
V-14/26.

139. CLOTH SASH

Cloth sash with geometric motifs and human faces. It fringes on the ends and in addition concave pieces of gold-plated silver are sewn on.

NAZCA

L: 179cm.
W: 8.6cm.
Museo "Oro del Perú"
V-58/02.

121

117

120

119

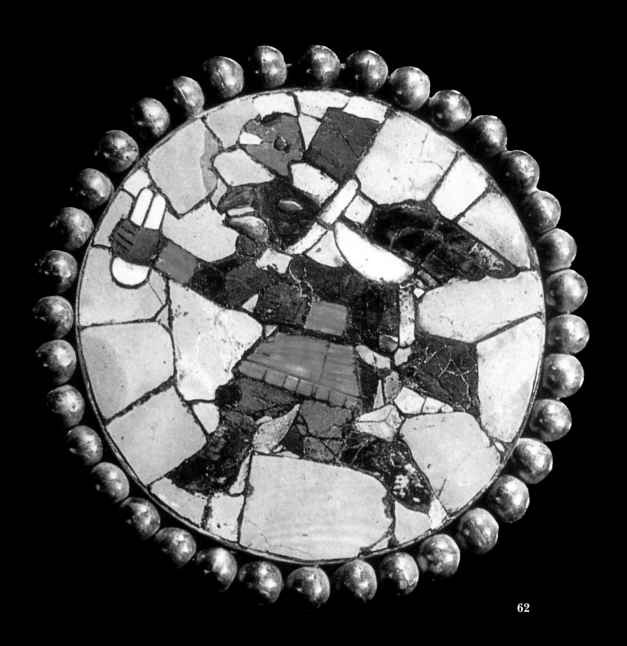

62

65

66

104

110

111

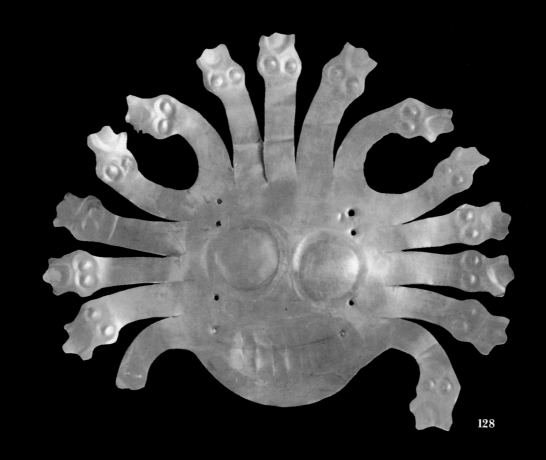

128

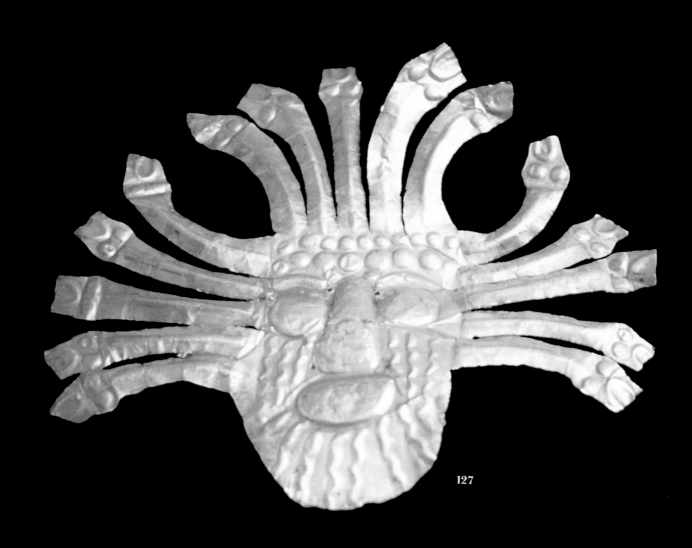

127

124

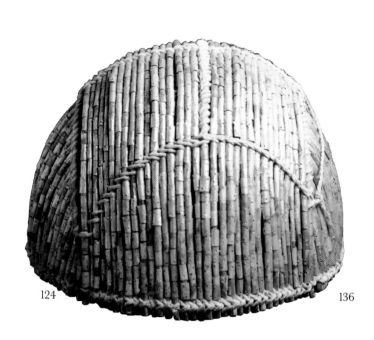

136

123

144 — 153

142 — 143

65

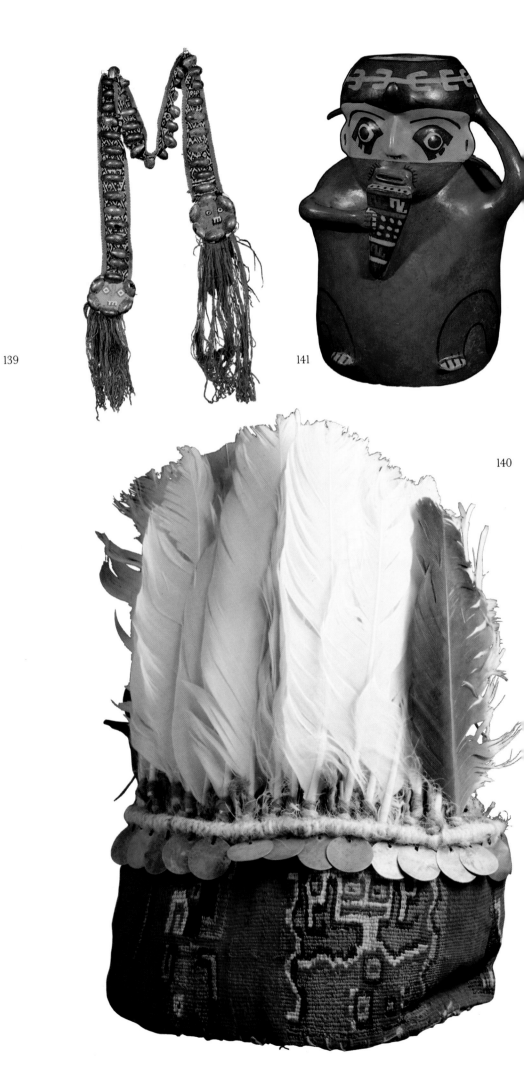

139

141

140

154

155

67

157

131

140. HEADDRESS

Headdress comprising a multi-coloured tapestry band with stylised human figures and other motifs. Attached to the upper border are 35 gold pendants, with feathers rising above them.

H: 26.5cm.
D: 15.5cm.
Museo "Oro del Perú"
V-46/18.

141. CERAMIC VESSEL

Ceramic vessel in the form of a human figure playing pan pipes. It is painted ochre, black, brown, cream and grey.

NAZCA (Coastal Wari?)

H: 29cm.
W: 18cm.
Museo "Oro del Perú"
V-22A/18.

142-144. MUMMIFIED HUMAN HAND WITH SCEPTRE AND BRACELET.

Mummified human hand wearing a gold bracelet and holding a gold sceptre. The bracelet is of corrugated sheet gold with bosses around the edges. The tubular sceptre has a spherical finial, ornamented with an open-work cross. Yellow cotton is wrapped round the elbow.

NAZCA

Museo "Oro del Perú"
V-42/6-7-8.

145-153. MUMMY

Male mummy with long hair, in seated position. Adorned with jewellery (not original to mummy).

NAZCA

GOLD BRACELET

Sheet-gold bracelet. Corrugated with bosses along edge.

L: 15.5cm.
W: 4.7cm.
Wt: 11.5g.

GOLD BRACELET

Sheet-gold bracelet. Corrugated with bosses along edge.

EARSPOOLS

Pair of gold earspools with decoration in relief. Perforations at centre.

D: 4.7cm.	*D:4.7cm.*
Wt: 5.5g	*Wt: 5.5g.*

PECTORAL

Comprising linked pieces of shell. Pendants of same material.

Nazca

GOLD LIP ORNAMENT

Lip ornament worked in high relief.

D: 1.5cm.
Wt: 50g.

HEADDRESS

Cloth and coloured feathers and ornamented with a strip of sheet gold with repoussé decoration

H: 5.5cm.
D: 19.0cm.
Wt: 42g.

NOSE ORNAMENT

Gold nose ornament with embossed decoration.

D: 3.3cm.
Wt: 1.5g.
Museo "Oro del Perú"
CUP-1.

154. CERAMIC VESSEL

Ceramic vessel in the shape of a parrot (macaw) with an oval body. Surmounted by a decorated handle and single tapering spout. The wings, head, and geometric designs of fish on the handle are depicted in grey, ochre, white/cream and outlined in black on a chestnut-red burnished surface.

NAZCA

H: 13cm.
W: 12.50cm.
L: 23cm.
British Museum
1938-18.

155. CERAMIC VESSEL

Double spout bridge-handled ceramic vessel with convex base. It depicts hummingbirds facing flowers which are at the base of the spouts. The designs are executed in grey, ochre, chestnut and outlined in black on a cream background.

NAZCA

H: 13.50cm.
Max.D: 11cm.
British Museum
1919.10.241.

156. GOLD MOUTH ORNAMENT

Sheet-gold repoussé crescentic mouth ornament with two extending appendages depicting snakes heads. One snake head is missing from the right-hand side "moustache", another on the left has been soldered back on.

NAZCA

H: 10.4cm.
W: 13.5cm.
Wt: 10.01g.
British Museum
1952 AM.10.1.

157. GOLD BRACELET

Sheet-gold bracelet with open ends, perforated towards the edges. It is decorated with ten repoussé feline motifs and stepped frets arranged in panels as part of a repeated design.

NAZCA

L: 9cm.
Max D: 6cm.
Min D: 5cm.
Wt: 36.45g.
British Museum
1921.3-21.1.

158. STONE CUP

Cup ornamented with coloured stones representing winged running warriors. There are circular incisions on the lower and upper parts of the cup.

TIAHUANACO

H: 10cm.
D: 7cm.
Wt: 356g.
Museo "Oro del Perú"
M3/393.

159. STONE CUP

Cup ornamented with coloured stones representing winged warriors running. There are incisions on the lower and upper ends of the cup.

TIAHUANACO

H: 9.8cm.
D: 7.3cm.
Wt: 350g.
Museo "Oro del Perú"
M3/375.

160. STONE LIME CONTAINER

Brown and beige fish-shaped stone lime container with chrysocolla eyes. It has stepped fret patterns and a double perforation on the upper body. Several types of stone have been used. Manufactured using a variety of techniques including drilling, incision, pecking and polishing.

TIAHUANACO

L: 10.5cm.
H: 4.5cm.
Wt: 222g.
Museo "Oro del Perú"
M2/197.

161. STONE LIME CONTAINER

Stone lime container in the shape of a zoomorphic figure with mother-of-pearl eyes. Several types of stone have been used. Manufactured using a variety of techniques including drilling, polishing, pecking, inlay and incision.

TIAHUANACO

H: 4.2cm.
W: 6.4cm.
L: 9cm.
Museo "Oro del Perú"
M3/478.

◬. *Tiahuanaco*

162. FRAGMENT OF STONE VASE

Fragment of polished andesite vase or beaker with a smooth inner surface and an outer surface with two registers ornamented in bas-relief. Snake/puma heads each contained within a square or curved frame.

TIAHUANACO

L: 11.5cm.
W: 1.5cm.
D: 7.5cm.
British Museum
1866.2-1.1.

163. CIRCULAR CERAMIC VESSEL

Circular doughnut-shaped ceramic vessel with spout. Two snakes are depicted in grey, black, chestnut and cream. They are outlined in black, or white on a burnished chestnut background. The short everted spout has decorations of chevrons in white, and chestnut outlined in black.

WARI (TIAHUANACO?)

H: 5cm.
   8 cm. with spout
Max D: 16 cm. (Outer)
Min D: 8 cm. (Inner)
British Museum
1954.W.A.M.138.

164. COTTON MANTLE

Dyed green cotton mantle with embroidered figures of birds and on either side a stepped fret with brown and red embroidery.

WARI

L: 1.64m.
W: 80cm.
Museo "Oro del Perú"

165. COTTON MANTLE

Cream-coloured cotton mantle with anthropomorphic and zoomorphic figures in red, blue, black and cream.

WARI

L: 1.50m.
W: 1.49m.
Museo "Oro del Perú"
PN/S/N.

166. CERAMIC VESSEL

Small portrait head vase with a flat base, depicting a finely modelled head wearing a red cap, with a small circular object on the chin and earspools in the earlobes. Ornamented with orange/ochre, red and black paints or slips, which have been burnished.

WARI (TIAHUANACO?)

H: 13cm.
Max.D: 12cm
Min D: 6cm.
British Museum
46.12-17.24.

167. GOLD BEAKER

Large gold beaker, with flaring sides ornamented with a repoussé design of three richly attired double-sceptered figures. Turquoise decorations are used for the headdress, breastplate, legs and upper part of the staff. Around the border there is a setting of turquoise discs. On the base there is relief decoration of an anthropo-zoomorphic figure and small circles.

CHIMU

H: 20cm.
D: 17.1cm.
Wt. 494.5g.
Museo "Oro del Perú"
V-76/02.

168. GOLD BEAKER

Gold beaker with flaring sides and a double bottom containing rattle pellets. The lower part has three openwork crosses, and the upper has four circular applications of chrysocolla contained within a border of small gold spheres. The motifs occupy a zone delimited by horizontal lines of small gold spheres.

CHIMU

H: 13.3cm.
D: 9.7cm.
Wt: 295g.
Museo "Oro del Perú"
V-76/29.

169. GOLD BEAKER

Gold beaker with flaring sides and a double bottom containing rattle pellets. The upper part has 4 circular pieces of chrysocolla inlay, while the lower part is decorated with openwork geometric designs.

CHIMU

H: 13.5cm.
D: 10cm.
Wt: 279g.
Museo "Oro del Perú"
V-76/26.

170. GOLD BEAKER

Large gold beaker with flaring sides. In the central part there is an inverted anthropomorphic face with large comma-shaped eyes, high relief nose and feline fangs, which retain traces of paint.

CHIMU

H: 25.8cm.
D: 20cm.
Wt: 815.5g.
Museo "Oro del Perú"
V-76/43.

171. GOLD BEAKER

Gold beaker with flaring sides. It has inverted anthropomorphic faces in relief on either side, with comma-shaped eyes and the teeth of carnivores. One of the faces retains traces of paint.

CHIMU

H: 13cm.
D: 11.9cm.
Wt: 168g.
Museo "Oro del Perú"
V-76/47.

172. GOLD AND SILVER BEAKER

Gold and silver beaker with flaring sides. It has inverted anthropomorphic faces in relief on either side, with feline teeth and comma-shaped eyes. The lower part, which is of silver, has a double base and openwork decoration. The upper part is gold.

CHIMU

H: 13.3cm.
D: 10.3cm.
Wt: 212g.
Museo "Oro del Perú"
V-83/07.

173. GOLD VESSEL

Double-spouted bridge-handled gold vessel, with flat pedestal base. The curved bridge has triangular and stepped decorations in openwork, and on top heads, with almond-shaped eyes, wearing semi-circular headdresses. These are repeated on the upper part of the body, while feline heads are placed near the base of each spout.

CHIMU

H: 22.8cm.
D: 23.5cm.
Wt: 593.5g.
Museo "Oro del Perú"
V-78/01.

174. GOLD AND SILVER DRINKING VESSEL

Double-spouted gold and silver vessel. Rhomboid-shaped body, central neck with slightly splayed sides, two conical spouts, and a plain pedestal base. The upper part of the body has heads in relief (three on each side) between bands of running scrolls. Two feline heads on the sides of the spouts.

CHIMU

H: 18.3cm.
D: 21.7cm.
Wt: 239g.
Museo "Oro del Perú"
V-83/08.

175. SILVER VESSEL

Double-spouted silver vessel. Pedestal base, curved bridge with openwork geometric decoration. The body and spout have embossed anthropo-zoomorphic figures, linked by continuous volutes. The upper part of the vessel has human figures with outstretched bodies in relief. Little monkeys hang on to the sides of the spouts, their tails on the body of the vessel.

CHIMU

H: 20.5cm.
D: 21cm.
Wt: 271.5g.
Museo "Oro del Perú"
V-86/35.

176. GOLD VESSEL

Double gold vessel. One part represents a figure wearing a headdress, with a head with almond-shaped eyes and features in relief. It has bent arms and legs. It is linked by a tube to a plain gold beaker with a flat base and flaring sides.

CHIMU

H: 14cm.
D: 18cm.
Wt: 361g.
Museo "Oro del Perú"
V-81/10.

177. GOLD AND SILVER VESSEL

Double vessel of gold and silver. One part is plain and has a flat base, while the other takes the shape of zoomorphic figures apparently engaged in erotic acts. One of the figures features earspools and a headdress. Both have circular inlays of chrysocolla, of which some are missing. The vessels are linked by a communicating tube.

CHIMU

H: 15cm.
L: 21.5cm.
Wt: 275g.
Museo "Oro del Perú"
V-81/22.

178. GOLD AND SILVER VESSEL

Double vessel of gold and silver. One part is in the shape of an anthropomorphic figure whose arms and legs are bent forward. The figure wears a conical headdress and has almond-shaped eyes, a circular nose and linear mouth. Disc-shaped inlaid chrysocolla adorns the ears and neck. A silver connecting tube provides the link with a gold beaker with a band of silver in the centre

CHIMU

H: 19cm.
L: 20cm.
Wt: 233g.
Museo "Oro del Perú"
V-81/25.

179. GOLD AND SILVER VESSEL

Conical vessel of alternate silver and gold elements, made up of three sheets of silver and three of gold.

CHIMU

H: 34.1cm.
D: 10.8cm.
Wt: 265.5g.
Museo "Oro del Perú"
V-83/11.

180. GOLD AND SILVER VESSEL

Conical vessel of alternate gold and silver elements, made up of three strips of silver and three of gold, with a gold rim. It is decorated with two moveable figures of birds, whose eyes are inlaid red shell beads. Gold discs are suspended from their beaks.

CHIMU

H: 32.7
D: 14.5cm.
Wt: 174g.
Museo "Oro del Perú"
V-69/26.

181. GOLD AND SILVER VESSEL

Gold and silver vessel with a double bottom containing rattle pellets. It comprises strips of silver and is decorated in relief with a gold anthropomorphic figure, with animal fangs, which lacks the lower part of one arm.

CHIMU

H: 15.2cm.
D: 10.5cm.
Wt: 137.5g.
Museo "Oro del Perú"
V-84/02.

182. GOLD VESSEL

Gold vessel with slightly flaring sides, a flat base and a central band of semi-repoussé panels ornamented with stylised birds.

CHIMU

H: 12.1cm.
D: 8.9cm.
Wt: 81g.
Museo "Oro del Perú"
V-70/15.

183. GOLD VESSEL

Gold vessel with a convex base, spherical body, slightly flaring neck and a straight bordered rim.

CHIMU

H: 15cm.
D: 8.2cm.
Wt: 161g.
Museo "Oro del Perú"
V-73/04.

164

165

158

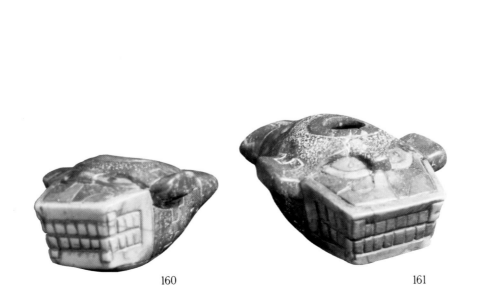

160

161

159

166

162

163

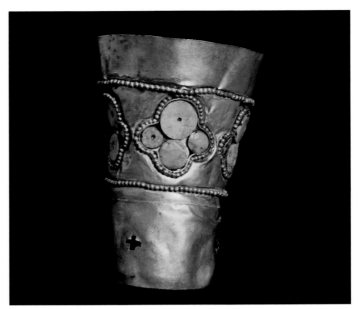

168

191

170

176

177

178

167

181

185

Chimú

184. GOLD VESSEL

Gold vessel with a splayed pedestal base, slightly flaring neck and added rim.

CHIMU

H: 15.5cm.
D: 11.8cm.
Wt: 215.4g.
Museo "Oro del Perú"
V-71/05.

185. GOLD AND SILVER VESSEL

Vessel of alternating gold and silver strips in the shape of a left lower leg. It has a silver foot with a gold sole and gold toenails hooked onto the toes.

CHIMU

H: 20.3cm.
D: 12cm.
Wt: 272g.
Museo "Oro del Perú"
V-84/19.

186. GOLD VESSEL

Gold vessel with a double bottom containing rattle pellets. Its body flares towards the mouth.

CHIMU

H: 25.1cm.
D: 13.7cm.
Wt: 160g.
Museo "Oro del Perú"
V-80/05.

187. GOLD VESSEL

Gold vessel in the shape of a bird, possibly a standing pigeon, with a tubular spout on its back. The eyes are inlaid with turquoise. A gold sphere is suspended from its beak.

CHIMU

H: 15cm.
L: 19.2cm.
Wt: 243.5g.
Museo "Oro del Perú"
V-79.03.

188. GOLD VESSEL

Gold vessel in the shape of a condor, with an oval body, convex base, head with beak, crest and neck feathers. One eye is of red shell, the other is missing. Wings with primary feathers and the tail are depicted. It has an everted spout (neck) on the back. Two gold strips have been added to the neck.

CHIMU

H: 12cm.
L: 20cm.
Wt: 150g.
Museo "Oro del Perú"
V-79/25.

189. GOLD BOWL

Gold bowl with a decoration in the shape of a bird on a flanged rim.

CHIMU

H: 8cm.
D: 15.2cm.
Wt: 100.5g.
Museo "Oro del Perú"
M4/26.

190. GOLD BEAKER

Gold beaker with a flat base and slightly flaring sides. Ornamented with repoussé designs of sea shells, birds and spears.

CHIMU

H: 14.5cm.
D of rim 10cm.
Wt: 104g.
Museo "Oro del Perú"
V-80/10.

191. GOLD MASK

Rectangular repoussé sheet-gold mask. It has almond eyes and a nose in high relief. There are traces of red paint on the face.

CHIMU

H: 16cm.
W: 25.5cm.
Wt: 30g.
Museo "Oro del Perú"
V-6/07.

192. GOLD MASK

Rectangular gold mask with comma-shaped eyes, repoussé mouth and nose in high relief. At either end and at the top and bottom it has trapezoidal pendants, which are suspended from hooks stapled onto the mask. There are traces of red paint on the face. Two pieces of chrysocolla provide pupils for the eyes.

CHIMU (Sicán Style)

H: 22.5cm.
W: 29.2cm.
Wt: 123g.
Museo "Oro del Perú"
V-10/45.

193. GOLD MASK

Rectangular gold mask made from a single sheet, with comma-shaped eyes, repoussé mouth and earspools, and a nose in high relief. There are embossed dots around the ears and earspools. Traces of red and green paint remain. Perforations on the ears, earspools and eyes.

CHIMU (Sicán Style)

H: 38.3cm.
W: 64.2 cm.
Wt: 120g.
Museo "Oro del Perú"
V-11/07.

194. GOLD TUMI (CEREMONIAL KNIFE)

Gold tumi containing rattle pellets. It has a trapezoidal handle and is surmounted by a richly-dressed human figure with comma-shaped eyes, nose in relief, arms bent forward, and a headdress with three appendages representing feathers or shells. The middle example is of chrysocolla. One earspool retains turquoise inlay. The back is decorated with geometrical and other designs.

CHIMU (Sicán Style)

H: 35.4cm.
W: 12.5cm.
Wt: 458g.
Museo "Oro del Perú"
V-18/18.

195. GOLD AND SILVER TUMI (CEREMONIAL KNIFE)

Gold and silver tumi, with two pigeon-shaped and three small bell-shaped pendants. The finial takes the shape of a human face wearing a headdress, framed by gold openwork. It has two turquoise earspools and five turquoises on the front of the headdress. On the reverse the headdress is ornamented with turquoise. The silver blade is overlaid in checkerboard fashion with gold foil. There are traces of fabric on the back.

CHIMU (Sicán Style)

H: 32.5cm.
W: 10.5cm.
Wt: 305g.
Museo "Oro del Perú"
V-30/05.

196. GOLD TUMI (CEREMONIAL KNIFE)

Gold tumi, the finial of which takes the form of a deer standing on a base. Twelve oval pendants are suspended from the base.

CHIMU

H: 30cm.
W: 10.5cm.
Wt: 288g.
Museo "Oro del Perú"
V-28/01.

197. GOLD AND SILVER TUMI (CEREMONIAL KNIFE)

Gold and silver tumi. The finial is an anthropomorphic head apparently representing a god. It is inlaid with turquoise.

§Chimú

CHIMU

H: 26.5cm.
W: 10.2cm.
Wt: 185g.
Museo "Oro del Perú"
V-21/02.

198. GOLD TUMI (CEREMONIAL KNIFE)

Gold tumi with openwork finial enclosed by bands of repoussé dots.

CHIMU

H: 24.1cm.
W: 13.4cm.
Wt: 177g.
Museo "Oro del Perú"
V-28/49.

199. GOLD AND SILVER TUMI (CEREMONIAL KNIFE)

Gold and silver tumi. The finial is an anthropomorphic head representing a Chimu god. A portion of the filigree decoration on the headdress is missing. The silver blade is overlaid in checkerboard fashion with gold foil. The surface is oxidised or burnt. There are traces of red paint on the reverse side of the finial.

CHIMU

H: 34cm.
W: 12.3cm.
Wt: 316g.
Museo "Oro del Perú"
V-32/02.

200. GOLD AND SILVER NECKLACE

Necklace with nine strands of gold, silver and pearl beads, bound together by transverse strands. Also, it has six pendants in the form of long irregular pearls. Restrung.

CHIMU

L: 55cm.
Wt: 135.5g.
Museo "Oro del Perú"
V-1/32.

201. GOLD AND AMETHYST NECKLACE

Necklace of rectangular and disc-shaped amethyst beads alternating with gold spheres. Restrung.

CHIMU

L: 38.5cm.
Wt: 185g.
Museo "Oro del Perú"
V-5/49.

Chimú

202. GOLD AND AMETHYST NECKLACE

Necklace of gold spheres alternating with amethyst beads of variable shape, which decrease in size towards the top.

CHIMU

L: 40.5cm.
Wt: 183g.
Museo "Oro del Perú"
V-8/20.

203. GOLD NECKLACE

Necklace of gold spheres and pendant pearls. Restrung.

CHIMU

L: 30cm.
Wt: 164g.
Museo "Oro del Perú"
V-8/40.

204. GOLD NECKLACE

Necklace of 34 large sheet-gold spheres. Restrung.

L: 52cm.
Wt: 178.5g.
Museo "Oro del Perú"
V-9/05.

205. GOLD NECKLACE

15-strand pearl necklace. They are of a standard size with the exception of the pendants, which are large, irregularly shaped and are held in place in a setting of semi-spheres of gold. Restrung.

CHIMU

L: 44.6cm.
Wt: 278g.
Museo "Oro del Perú"
V-23/48.

206. GOLD NECKLACE

Necklace of 12 strands of miniature links or gold spheres. Restrung.

CHIMU

L: 54cm.
Wt: 172.5g.
Museo "Oro del Perú"
V-9/16.

207. GOLD AND TOPAZ NECKLACE

Necklace of gold spheres and topaz beads. The beads vary in shape, decreasing in size towards the top. Restrung.

CHIMU

L: 41.5cm.
Museo "Oro del Perú"
V-8/15.

208. GOLD NECKLACE

Double-strand necklace of graduated gold beads representing fish vertebrae. Restrung.

CHIMU

L: 36cm.
Wt: 154g.
Museo "Oro del Perú"
V-13/23.

209. GOLD, LAPIS LAZULI AND TURQUOISE NECKLACE

Necklace of spheres of gold, and beads of turquoise, chrysocolla and lapis lazuli. Restrung.

CHIMU

L: 47cm.
Museo "Oro del Perú"
V-24/45.

210. GOLD AND AMETHYST NECKLACE

Necklace of alternating gold and amethyst beads. The amethysts are of different sizes and shapes - spherical, tubular and oval. The largest beads are in the central section of the necklace. Restrung.

CHIMU

L: 39cm.
Wt: 254g.
Museo "Oro del Perú"
V-24/30.

211. GOLD AND EMERALD NECKLACE

Necklace of gold spheres and emeralds. The eight emeralds occur towards the bottom and form part of a pendant. Restrung.

CHIMU

L: 40cm.
Wt: 71.5g.
Museo "Oro del Perú"
V-24/42.

212. GOLD AND TURQUOISE BRACELET

Gold and turquoise bracelet. Formed of gold discs, encircled by spheres, in the centre of which are small turquoise discs. It is attached to a cloth backing.

CHIMU

L: 20cm.
W: 2.5cm.
Wt: 57.5g.
Museo "Oro del Perú"
V-22/56.

213-214. GOLD EARSPOOLS

Pair of gold earspools. Concave discs, the inner parts which are ornamented with filigree in geometric and volute patterns. The filigree is encircled by small gold spheres. Central turquoises are held in place from behind by crossed bands. The backs are flanged. Incomplete.

CHIMU

213   D: 8.2cm.   214   D: 8.2cm.
     Wt: 54g.   *Wt: 48g.*
Museo "Oro del Perú"
V-10/05-06.

215-216. GOLD EARSPOOLS

Pair of gold earspools. Concave discs, the inner parts of which are ornamented with openwork depicting zoomorphic figures separated by transverse strips. The openwork is contained within circles of small gold spheres. Central turquoises are held in place from behind by crossed bands. Incomplete.

CHIMU

215   D: 8cm.   216   D: 8.2cm
     Wt: 63.5g.   *Wt: 60.5g.*
Museo "Oro del Perú"
V-10/19-20.

217-218. GOLD EARSPOOLS

Pair of gold earspools. Each is made of two discs linked by a central cylindrical tube and a sheet of gold soldered to the outer ring. The centres are ornamented with stepped fret openwork contained within rings of beading. In the middle, further beading encloses turquoises.

CHIMU

217   D: 6.8cm.   218   D: 6.8cm.
     Wt: 61g.   *Wt: 61g.*
Museo "Oro del Perú"
V-10/23-24.

219-220. GOLD EARSPOOLS

Pair of disc-shaped gold earspools. Within plain gold borders, mosaics of stones and shells represent human standing figures, with open arms, faces in relief and wearing semi-circular headdresses.

CHIMU

219   D: 8.8cm.   220   D: 8.8cm.
     Wt: 96g   *Wt: 90g.*
Museo "Oro del Perú"
V-10/41-42.

221-222. GOLD ROUNDELS

Pair of gold roundels from earspools. Encircled by beading and within plain borders, they are ornamented with openwork and stepped fret designs.

CHIMU

221   D: 9.7cm.   222   D: 9.7cm.
     H: 1.3cm.   *H: 1.3cm.*
     Wt: 42.5g.   *Wt: 44.5g*
Museo "Oro del Perú"
V-10/27-28.

Chimú

223. GOLD CROWN

Sheet-gold crown in the form of a tall, waisted cylinder. Decorated with pairs of stylised birds contained in alternating panels, their bodies outlined by clusters of small bosses. The gold sheet is fastened with staples.

CHIMU

H: 19cm.
D: 19cm.
Wt: 347g.
Museo "Oro del Perú"
V-13/38.

224. GOLD CROWN

Sheet-gold crown in the form of a tall, wasited cylinder. Ornamented in relief in three horizontal bands, the upper and lower of which have rows of birds. The wide central band has zoomorphic figures, triangles and diamonds. Tiny bosses fill the background in all the panels. The gold sheet is fastened with staples.

CHIMU

H: 20cm.
D: 21.5cm.
Wt: 253.5g.
Museo "Oro del Perú"
V-9/42.

225. GOLD CROWN

Sheet-gold crown in the form of a tall cylinder. The surface is decorated with openwork zoomorphic subjects. It has seven plumes; the central one takes the shape of a semi-circular blade (tumi) with bosses round the edges.

CHIMU

H: 40cm.
D: 18.5cm.
Wt: 439g. (including consolidating material)
Museo "Oro del Perú"
V-18/09.

226. GOLD CROWN

Cylindrical gold crown with attached tall plume. Both crown and plume are richly decorated with circular bosses.

CHIMU

D: 18cm.
H: 14.8cm. (without plume)
H: 38.5cm. (with plume)
Wt: 194.5g. (with acrylic support)
Museo "Oro del Perú"
V-37/04.

188

187

195

245

203

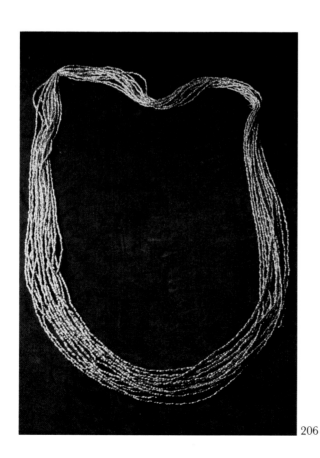

206

204

215 216

224 223

225

92

227. GOLD BOX

Cylindrical gold box with a lid of the same shape and a small central ring. Plain base and straight sides. Damaged.

CHIMU

H: 14.2cm.
D: 18.5cm.
Wt: 856.5g.
Museo "Oro del Perú"
V-36/01.

228. GOLD SPATULA

Long trapezoidal gold spatula. The finial is a human figure, with comma-shaped eyes, wearing a headdress and apparently holding spheres.

CHIMU

H: 19.8cm.
W: 4.1cm.
Wt: 18g.
Museo "Oro del Perú"
V-36/02.

229. GOLD SCEPTRE

Gold sceptre with pendants and repoussé work representing crabs, shrimps, and molluscs.

CHIMU

H: 56.6cm.
W: 7.5cm.
Wt: 90.5g.
Museo "Oro del Perú"
V-11/54.

230. GOLD TWEEZERS

Gold tweezers ornamented with a stylised bird against a background of tiny bosses. Perforation at top.

CHIMU

L: 11cm.
W: 9cm.
Wt: 59g.
Museo "Oro del Perú"
V-19/84.

231. GOLD AND SILVER NOSE ORNAMENT

Gold and silver nose ornament in the form of a human face with a headdress. The repoussé face is of oxidised or burnt silver. The headdress, with two diverging appendages, is gold. There is an oval aperture at the top centre of the headdress. Traces of red paint survive on the back.

CHIMU

H: 9.5cm.
W: 12cm.
Wt: 18.5g.
Museo "Oro del Perú"
V-42/01.

232. CERAMIC SEA SHELL WITH GOLD

Burnished black ceramic seashell, adorned with a ribbon of gold. It has four perforations and incised geometric patterns.

CHIMU

L: 14cm.
W: 7cm.
Wt: 148.5g.
Museo "Oro del Perú"
V-24/12.

233. GOLD SEASHELL

Seashell made of three pieces of sheet gold. There are two perforations towards the top.

CHIMU

L: 17cm.
W: 4.8cm.
Wt: 73g.
Museo "Oro del Perú"
V-24/11.

234. PIECE OF GOLD

Gold nugget, in natural state, with quartz (inclusion).

CHIMU

L: 6.4cm.
W: 3.8cm.
H: 2.8cm.
Wt: 149g.
Museo "Oro del Perú"
V-58/08.

235. PIECE OF GOLD

Piece of cast (smelted) gold.

CHIMU

W: 3.9cm.
H: 0.4cm.
Wt: 149g.
Museo "Oro del Perú"
V-58/19.

236. PIECE OF GOLD

Piece of cast gold.

CHIMU

W: 5.2cm.
H: 0.5cm.
Wt: 179.5g.
Museo "Oro del Perú"
V-58/20.

237. GILDED SILVER PECTORAL

Made of four rectangular strips of gilded silver which have been joined together. The upper end is convex and the lower part ends in two strips. It is decorated with patterns of small hemispherical bosses.

CHIMU

H: 86cm.
W: 41cm.
Museo "Oro del Perú"
V-9/36.

238. FEATHER PONCHO

Woven cotton poncho with multi-coloured feathers attached.

CHIMU

W: 35.5cm.
L: 56cm.
Museo "Oro del Perú"
COS V-55.

239. FEATHER PONCHO

Woven cotton poncho with green, black and white feathers attached.

CHIMU

L: 77cm.
W: 69cm.
Museo "Oro del Perú"
COS V-53.

240. SMALL PONCHO

Small poncho of light ochre cotton. Ornamented with cut-out gold foil geometric and wave motifs, interspersed with embossed human heads, birds and discs, some of burnished gold, the others matt. Arrangement of decoration is hypothetical.

CHIMU

L: 51cm.
W: 31cm.
Museo "Oro del Perú"
V-52/04.

241. BREASTPLATE

Breastplate with rectangular plaques of mother-of-pearl fastened to a textile backing. Gold discs are attached to the outer edges and between them and the mother-of-pearl plaques are traces of coloured feathers.

CHIMU

H: 45cm.
W: 38cm.
Museo "Oro del Perú"
V-56/22.

242. GOLD TUNIC

Tunic covered with small square plates of gold foil, each with four perforations. Brown and cream coloured tassels form a fringe around the edges of the sleeves and collar.

CHIMU

H: 60cm.
L: 155cm.
Museo "Oro del Perú"
V-59/01.

243. CLOTH AND GOLD PONCHO

§Chimú

Cloth and gold poncho, with repoussé, embossed and open work decoration. Anthropomorphic, ornithomorphic, geometric and other figures, are sewn onto the cloth. On the reverse there is also a sheet of gold, with mythological, geometric and running scroll motifs.

CHIMU

L: 50cm.
W: 31cm.
Museo "Oro del Perú"
V-52/04.

244. GOLD SPEAR

Spear (or ceremonial digging staff) with lozenge-shaped head. Made of embossed sheet gold over wood, with a long copper point at the base of the shaft. The head is decorated with pairs of stylised human figures facing each other and wearing domed headdress with plumes, while at its base is a head wearing a similar headdress and earspools.

CHIMU

H: 25.1cm
W: 17.5cm.
Museo "Oro del Perú"
V-11/04.

245. SILVER DISC

Silver disc with a central boss and ornamented with four concentric bands of complex embossed designs. Incomplete.

CHIMU

D: 34.8cm.
Wt: 158g.
Museo "Oro del Perú"
V-85/01.

246. WOODEN OAR OR TILLER

Wooden oar or tiller, decorated on one side of the blade with pelicans and a stepped fret pattern. The upper part is painted and is surmounted by a bar ornamented with four carved openwork pelicans. Alternatively, may have been a grave marker.

CHIMU

L: 201cm.
W: 24.5cm.
Museo "Oro del Perú"

247. WOODEN OAR OR TILLER

Wooden oar or tiller. The blade is ornamented with two openwork birds (egrets or possibly pelicans) and surmounted by a cylindrical stem with a finial of a single open cut bird, which has traces of red, cream, ochre and and black paint. Alternatively, may have been a grave marker.

CHIMU

L: 185cm.
W: 21.5cm.
Museo "Oro del Perú"

248. LITTER

Back-rest of wooden litter. The rear elevation is richly ornamented with six large portals (arranged in upper and lower rows of three) and, on either side, a small double portal. They are decorated with paint, sheet gold and metal pendants. The large portals enclose three fully-dressed figures and the smaller portals single figures. Single figures also stand between the portals in the upper row. At the base are support rods.

CHIMU (reputedly from Chan Chan)

W: 63cm.
L: 129cm.
Museo "Oro del Perú"
5745.

249. CERAMIC VESSEL

Burnished black ceramic vessel in the shape of a deer head. It has a plain rim. There is a perforation in the right ear.

CHIMU

H: 13cm.
L: 17cm.
D of base: 9.3cm.
Museo "Oro del Perú"
V-12A/2.

250. CERAMIC VESSEL

Ceramic vessel in the shape of two linked adult pelicans. One has an infant pelican on its back and the other a spout, both of which are connected by a bridge handle. Ornamented with chestnut red and cream slips (or paint). It whistles when filled with liquid.

CHIMU

H: 17.2cm.
L: 16.3cm.
Museo "Oro del Perú"
V-11A/12.

251. GOLD BEAKER

Sheet-gold beaker with everted bevelled rim and a concave base. The face on the centre of the vessel has a beaked nose, embossed ears, nose and eyes, and a geometric fish-like design on the reverse representing hair.

CHIMU (Ica?)

H: 19.1cm.
Max D: 7.1cm.
Min D: 6.2cm.
Wt: 95.15g.
British Museum
1933.7 - 13.154.

252. GOLD VASE

Gold vase with everted lip with a raised band under the rim. The base has been burnished with a small tool.

CHIMU (possibly Inca from Ecuador)

H: 13.5cm.
Max D: 11.2cm.
Min D: 6.7cm.
Wt: 163.85g.
British Museum
1907.3 - 19.536.

§Chimú

253-254. GOLD EARSPOOLS

Pair of convex gold disc earspools with wire mesh "open work" centres. The central rods or stems are of silver soldered on to the backs of the discs.

CHIMU

253 D:3.6cm.	254 D:3.6cm.
Wt: 10.54g.	Wt: 10.54g.

British Museum
1920.10-13 (4a)-(4b).

255-256. GOLD EARSPOOLS

Pair of convex sheet-gold earspools with discs depicting stylised repoussé birds surrounded by stipple and outlined with incised lines. On the reverse are points of solder where the stems or posts have been broken off.

CHIMU

255 D:3cm.	256 D:3cm.
W: 0.4cm.	W: 0.5cm.
Wt: 4.01g.	Wt: 4.01g.

British Museum
1920.10 - 13 (3a)-(3b).

257-258. GOLD EARSPOOLS

Pair of convex sheet-gold earspools with discs depicting stylised repoussé birds surrounded by dots and stipple and outlined with incised lines. The earspool stems are hollow cylinders of silver which rattle. There is evidence of thread around the stems.

CHIMU (Ica)

257 D: 4.2cm.	258 D: 4.2cm.
W: 2.2cm.	W: 2.2cm.
Wt: 8.75g.	Wt: 8.64g

British Museum
1920.10-13(2a)-(2b).

259. GOLD HAIR ORNAMENT

Circular gold hair ornament with two circles of repoussé bosses around a grinning face. The central element is surmounted by a divided strip (feathers?) and a tapering spoke below. The disc has a damaged edge.

CHIMU (Huacho)

L: 23.7cm.
W: 6.2cm.
Wt: 6.82g.
British Museum
1913.10-20.2.

260. CERAMIC VESSEL

Ceramic pedestal whistling vessel in the shape of a reed boat (caballito), with two squatting figures connected by a bridge handle. The design includes birds, fish, nets and reeds in chestnut-red and sepia paint on a cream slip base, painted in a cursive style.

CHIMU

H: 19.50cm.
L: 21cm.
W: 10cm.
D: 8cm.
British Museum
1921.10.27.28.

261. DRUM

Leather drum with a reed framework. A cylindrical body ornamented with semi-circular geometric designs, zigzags, waves and parallel lines. The front is painted with a human figure wearing a semi-circular headdress. The colours used are black, reddish-pink, white and brown.

CHANCAY

H: 12cm.
D: 26cm.
Museo "Oro del Perú"
V-32/14.

262. BAG (CHUSPA)

Cloth bag with 48 repoussé sheet-gold squares attached. The handle and edges are made of various coloured beads (chaquira). Apparently it was used for coca.

CHANCAY

W: 21.5cm.
H: 17cm.
Museo "Oro del Perú"
V-56/03.

263. TUNIC

Brown cotton warp-weave tunic with red, yellow and black decorated border with fringes. The breast, sleeves and hem are decorated with concave gold and keyhole shaped decorations and miniature bells.

CHANCAY

W: 150cm. (including sleeves)
L: 137cm.
Museo "Oro del Perú"
V-52/01.

264. GAUZE

Quadrangular yellow gauze with applied decorations of birds, distributed in horizontal and vertical lines.

CHANCAY

H: 79cm.
W: 87cm.
Museo "Oro del Perú"
S-V-81.

265. GAUZE

Quadrangular white gauze with applied decorations in the form of birds, distributed in horizontal and vertical lines.

CHANCAY

H: 85cm.
W: 93cm.
Museo "Oro del Perú"
S-V-83.

Chancay

266-274. FUNERARY MUMMY BUNDLE

Mummy bundle adorned with jewellery. The false head has silver decorations in the eyes and nose. It is accompanied by bundles of weaving materials of different colours and on the back a series of packages.

CHANCAY

Overall H: 102cm.
Overall W: 64cm.

SILVER HEADBAND

Decorated with repoussé anthropomorphic figures.

W: 4.8cm.
L: 31cm.

WOODEN EARSPOOLS

Pair of wooden earspools with mother-of-pearl inlay. Ornamented at the centre with human heads with chrysocolla eyes and wearing headdressses.

L: 3.2cm.	L: 3.2cm.
D: 4.8cm.	D: 4.9cm.

SILVER PECTORAL

Crescent-shaped with repoussé-decoration including a human face at the centre. Bird-shaped pendants are suspended from either end.

L: 20cm.
W: 5cm.
Wt: 12g.

SILVER NECKLACE

Necklace of silver spheres. Restrung.

L: 42.5cm.
W: 160 gm.

GOLD NECKLACE

Necklace of gold spheres. Restrung.

L: 43cm.
Wt: 41.5g.

SILVER NECKLACE

Necklace of rhomboidal silver beads. Restrung.

L: 34.5cm.
Wt: 39g.

SEED NECKLACE

Seed necklace. Restrung.

L: 33cm.
Museo "Oro del Perú"
CUP/3.

275. CERAMIC IDOL

Ceramic idol in the shape of a female figure with outstretched arms. Painted black and red.

CHANCAY

H: 38cm.
W: 27.5cm.
Museo "Oro del Perú"
V-13/05.

226

221

222

248

97

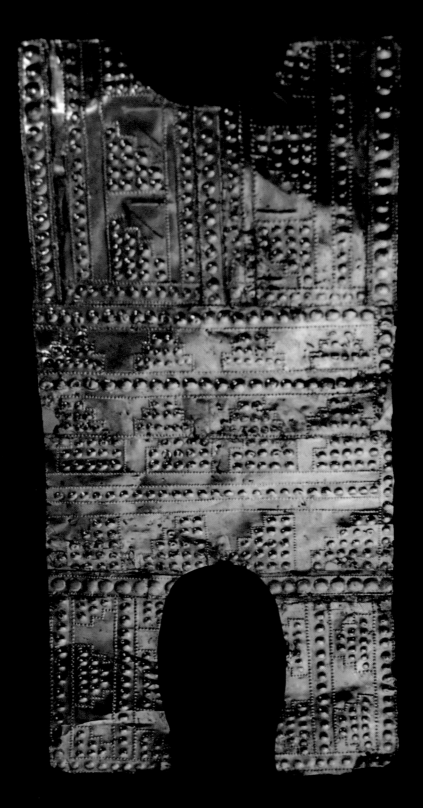

237

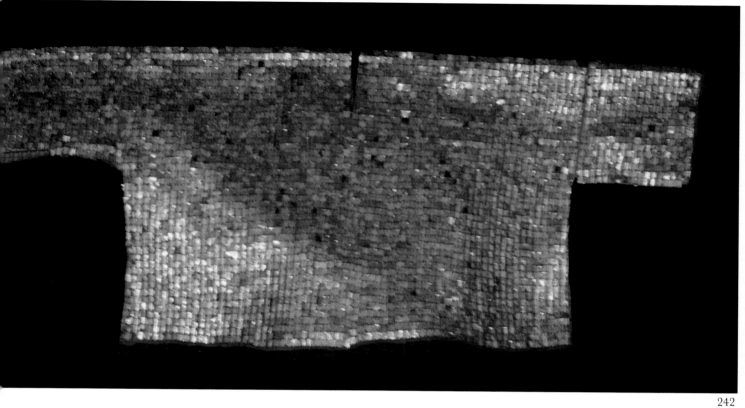

242

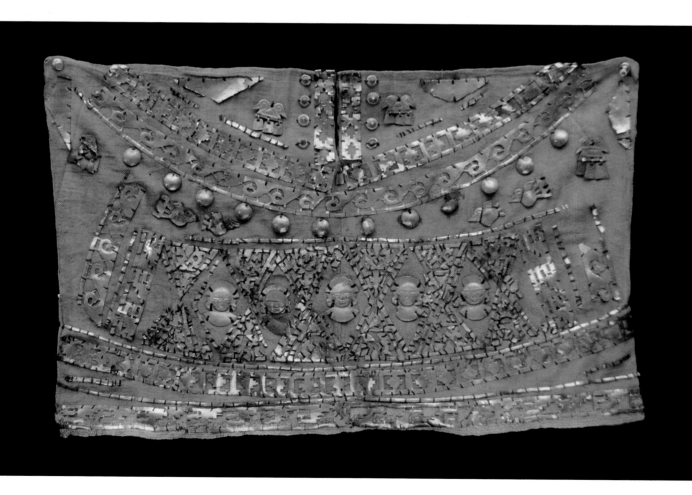

240

99

250

241

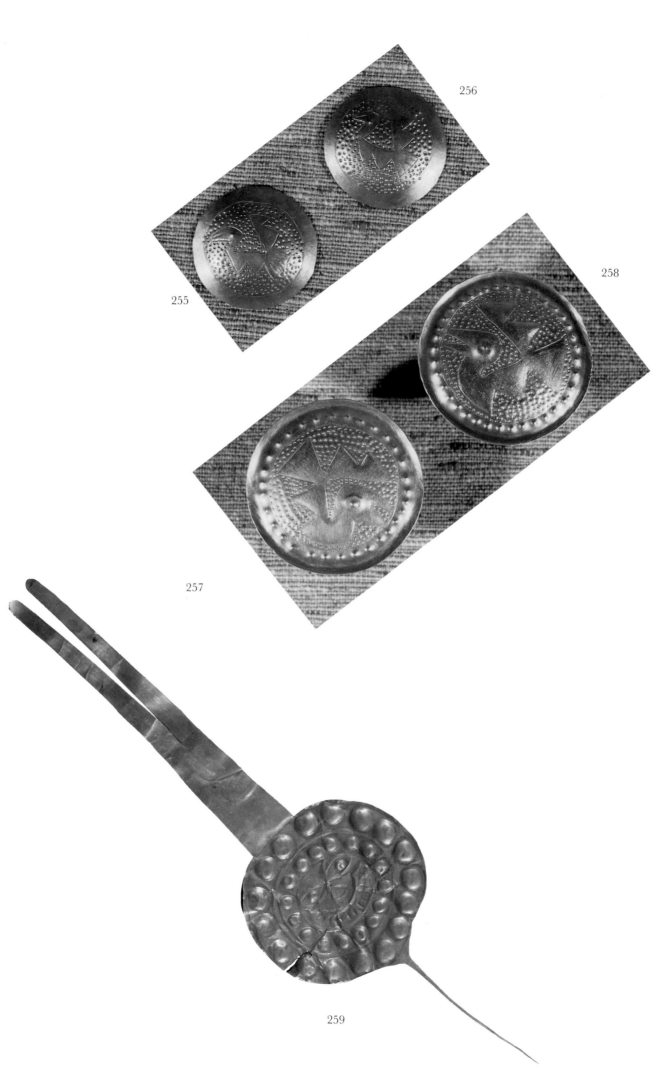

256

255

258

257

259

260

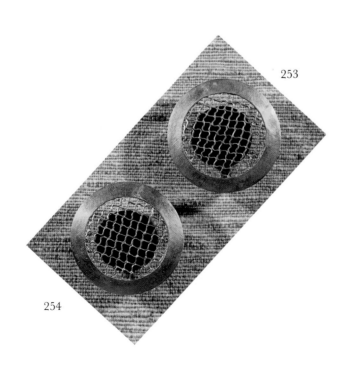

253

254

266 — 274

261

104

280   281

289

291   294   293   292

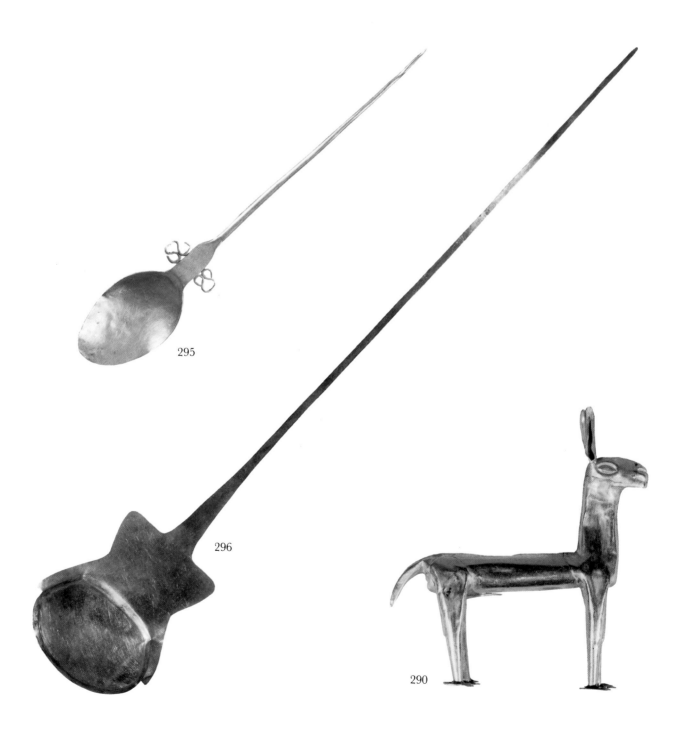

295

296

290

299

107

276. CERAMIC IDOL

Ceramic idol in the shape of a male figure with outstretched arms and wearing a headdress. Painted red and black.

CHANCAY

H: 40cm.
W: 26cm.
Museo "Oro del Perú"
V-13/08.

277. CERAMIC VESSEL

Vase with a long, slightly everted, neck connected to handles on a lentoid body. Decorated with geometrical textile designs in several registers and colours red, black, ochre and chestnut, and a series of birds depicted in a curvilinear style within a band. The neck and spout are black.

ICA

H: 18cm.
Max: D: 16cm.
Min D: 5.3cm.
British Museum
R.1933.7-13.21.

278-279. SMALL GOLD CUPS

Pair of miniature cups of sheet gold with slightly flaring sides and flat everted rims. Below the rim, and contained within horizontal bands, they have repoussé geometric decorations.

INCA

278 H: 3.8cm.   279 H: 3.7cm.
     D: 4.2cm.   D: 4.1cm.
     Wt: 15.5g.   Wt: 15.5g.
Museo "Oro del Perú"
V-87/309-310.

280. GOLD MALE FIGURINE

Standing gold male figurine with arms over its abdomen, face modelled in relief, conical headdress, extended earlobes and an erect genital organ.

INCA

H: 11.8cm.
W: 3.5cm.
Wt: 28.5g.
Museo "Oro del Perú"
V-33/66.

281. GOLD FEMALE FIGURINE

Standing gold female figurine with hands on the abdomen, and face and hair outlined in relief.

INCA

H: 10.5cm.
W: 3.2cm.
Wt: 23g.
Museo "Oro del Perú"
V-33/65.

282. GOLD MALE FIGURINE

Gold male figurine with hands on the abdomen. It also has earspools and a headdress. There are single perforations in the feet.

Ica ⁑ Inca

INCA

H: 12.5cm.
W: 4.5cm.
Wt: 37g.
Museo "Oro del Perú"
V-33/64.

283. GOLD FEMALE FIGURINE

Gold female figurine with hands on the abdomen. Hair with a central parting. There are single perforations in the feet.

INCA

H: 12.5cm.
W: 4cm.
Wt: 35.5g.
Museo "Oro del Perú"
V-33/63.

284. GOLD FEMALE FIGURINE

Gold female figurine with arms bent towards the chest. The face is outlined in high relief and the hair drawn back with decorative combs.

INCA

H: 15.1cm.
W: 3.5cm.
Wt: 101g.
Museo "Oro del Perú"
V-33/67.

285. GOLD LLAMA

Standing gold llama, face modelled in relief. The eyes and the snout are outlined.

INCA

H: 6.1cm.
W: 4.6cm.
Wt: 10.5g.
Museo "Oro del Perú"
V-33/93.

286. GOLD LLAMA

Standing gold llama with head modelled in relief. The eyes and snout are outlined but the ears are missing.

INCA

H: 4.5cm.
W: 4.5cm.
Wt: 9g.
Museo "Oro del Perú"
V-33/95.

287. WOODEN KERO (CEREMONIAL CUP)

Wooden kero with flaring sides, painted with a figure of a warrior brandishing a spear and a shield, under a rainbow. Around the centre is a band of stepped fret designs, and below this representations of the cantuta flower. The decoration is painted in red, yellow and green.

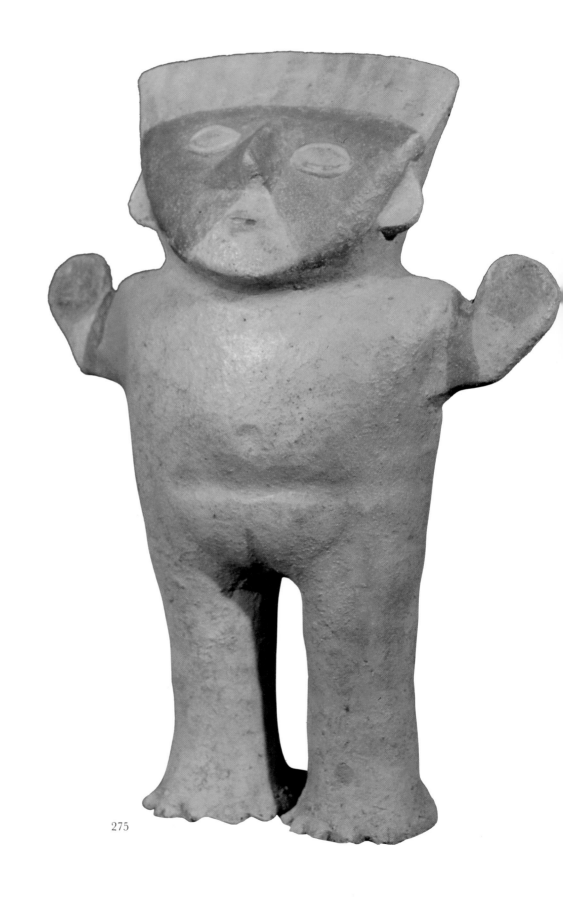

275

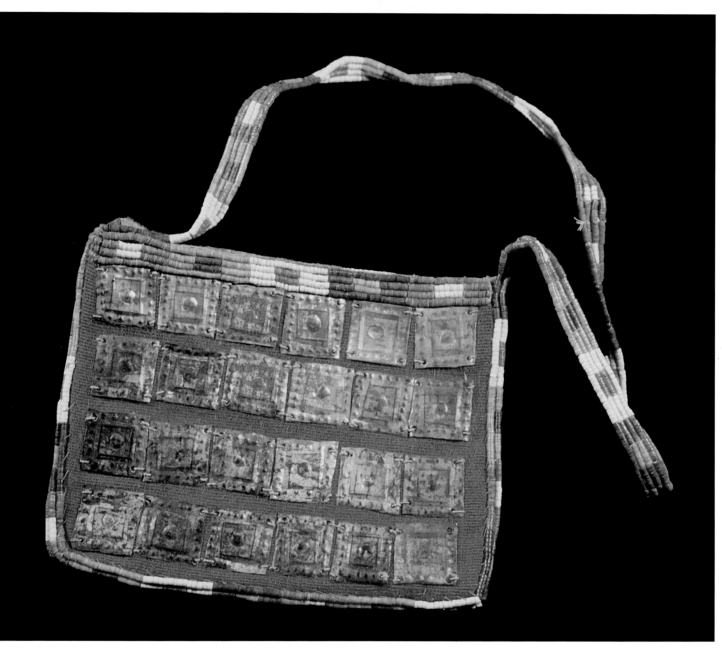

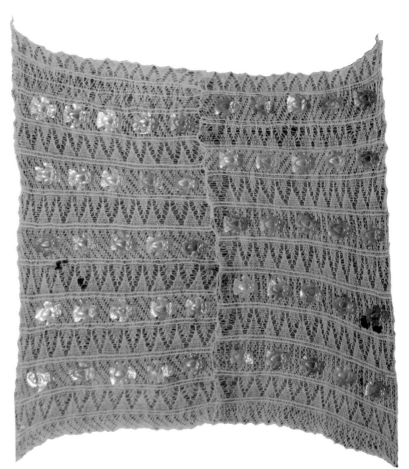

264

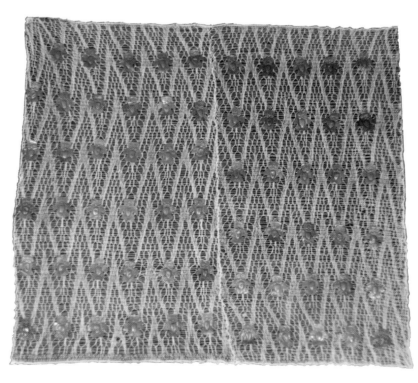

265

INCA

H: 18cm.
D: 16cm.
Wt: 651g.
Museo "Oro del Perú"
V-22/27.

288 WOODEN KERO (CEREMONIAL CUP)

Wooden kero decorated with incised rhomboidal shapes. It is painted brown, yellow and red.

INCA

H: 20cm.
D: 17cm.
Wt: 831g.
Museo "Oro del Perú"
V-22/28.

289. WOODEN KERO (CEREMONIAL CUP)

Wooden kero in the shape of a jaguar head. It is painted boldly in yellow, white, black, green and red.

INCA

H: 14cm.
D: 8cm.
Wt: 592g.
Museo "Oro del Perú"
V-22/32.

290. GOLD LLAMA

Sheet-gold male llama with modelled head, tubular ears, conical tail, tapering legs attached to webbed feet and a cylindrical body. Made in several pieces, with fine soldered joins.

INCA

H: 6.5cm.
L: 6cm.
W: 1cm.
Wt: 9.48g.
British Museum
1921.7-21.1.

291. GOLD FEMALE FIGURINE

Small hollow gold female standing figurine with hands on abdomen. The eyes, nose and hair are modelled. There is a hole under the chin. The figure lacks feet. It is probably made with thin gold/silver alloy pressed sheets.

INCA

H: 5.7cm.
W: 1.5cm.
Wt: 10.4g.
British Museum
7082.

292. GOLD FEMALE FIGURINE

Small hollow gold standing female figurine, modelled in relief. The hair, eyes and fingers are indicated by incised lines. The feet are not modelled, but are made from flat sheets. Made in two pieces.

INCA

H: 5.7cm.
W: 1.6cm.
Wt: 8.05g.
British Museum
1927.10.7-6.

293. GOLD MALE FIGURINE

Small hollow gold male standing figurine with hands on abdomen. The almond-shaped eyes, nose and mouth are modelled as is the single soldered strip earlobes and the tapering cap. The figure is made from soldered gold alloy.

INCA

L: 5.2cm.
W: 1.6cm.
Wt: 7.82g.
British Museum
1847.5-27.2.

294. GOLD FIGURE

Miniature cast gold crouching figure with hands over chest and hemispherical helmet/headdress. It has a highly polished surface, some discolouration in the areas of low relief. There are file marks on the base of the feet.

INCA?

L: 2.7cm.
W: 1.2cm.
Wt: 19.05g.
British Museum
1933.7 - 13.162.

295. TUPU (GOLD CLOAK PIN)

Spoon-shaped gold cloak pin, or tupu, with wire decorative hooks attached with silver coloured solder on either side of the stem immediately above the bowl. The handle tapers to a point.

INCA (Possibly Colonial)

L: 15.4cm.
W: 2.5cm.
Wt: 15.08g
British Museum
1928.6-6.2.

296. TUPU (GOLD CLOAK PIN)

Flat gold cloak pin, or tupu, with a large circular depression at the end (possibly meant to hold an ornamental inlay). The flat hammered stem tapers to a point.

Inca

INCA

L: 30.8cm.
W: 5.2cm.
Wt: 24.11g.
British Museum
1844.7-29.1.

297. STONE VESSEL

Stone vessel (andesite?) with 2 perforated lugs. There are 10 stylised snakes on outer edges, rim and lugs. Two of the snakes form spirals.

INCA

H: 16cm.
Inner D: 34cm.
Max.D: 43cm.
British Museum
1909.4-3.1.

298. STONE VESSEL

Polished basalt container in the shape of a stylised alpaca. There is a large perforation on the back. The tail, "mane" and ears are sketchily represented. It has a round body with a flat base.

INCA

H: 8.3cm.
L: 10.5cm.
W: 4.7cm.
British Museum
1933. 3-15.38.

299. WOODEN KERO (CEREMONIAL CUP)

Polished kero *with painted or "lacquered" designs in two registers. The upper register depicts a procession of Inca peoples, one bearing a flag, a Spaniard and a Negro. The lower register depicts a feline creature with flowers or fruit above it and an emblem to the right. The design is painted in red, green and cream on a red background.*

INCA/COLONIAL

H: 21cm.
Max. D: 18cm.
Min. D: 13cm.
British Museum
1950.AM.22.1.

300. CERAMIC VESSEL

Pottery paccha, *in the form of an aryballus, maize cob and digging stick. Possibly a water (chicha) vessel used in connection with agricultural ceremonies. The aryballus is ornamented with geometrical designs in sepia and brown.*

INCA

H: 42cm.
W: 18cm.
British Museum
1947 AM.10.39.

ACKNOWLEDGEMENTS

According to Inca legend, gold and silver were "the sweat of the sun and the tears of the moon". It is fitting that part of that lyrical phrase has been incorporated in the title of this major exhibition. The bulk of the exhibits have come from the Museo "Oro del Perú", Lima. Although it is a private foundation, the museum's rich collection is regarded as a Peruvian national treasure. Consequently, we have not only to express our deep gratitude to the museum's director, Victoria Mujica de Perez Palacio, for agreeing to bring a selection of the best pieces to Edinburgh but also to the Peruvian Government for authorising their temporary export. In addition, thanks are due to the Trustees of the British Museum for agreeing to lend items from the Museum of Mankind to supplement the exhibits from Lima.

During the course of our negotiations to secure the exhibition, we received considerable help from the staff of the British Embassy in Lima and from the British Council Representative there and his colleagues. I am happy to record our debt to them.

Large events of this nature are expensive to organise and publicise. On behalf of Edinburgh District Council, I should like to acknowledge the generous assistance which has been received from The Scotsman, Nimmo Colour Printers, Eastern Scottish Omnibuses, Ads Anker Data Systems, Scot Rail, Security Express and Expocolour.

A number of individuals and organisations have contributed to this venture. From an early stage considerable encouragement and practical advice was received from Elizabeth Carmichael of the Museum of Mankind. Dr. Warwick Bray, the author of the introductory article on pre-Hispanic metalwork, has been generous with his time. Two research assistants, Dr. W. Iain Mackay and S. Anita Schrader, employed to provide specialist expertise, have worked well beyond the call of duty. Also, the Lothian and Borders Police have earned our gratitude for wide-ranging assistance.

The exhibition has enjoyed the support of Councillor Paolo Vestri, Convener, Recreation Committee, Roger Jones, Director of Recreation, and our colleagues in the Marketing Section of the Recreation Department. The staff of the Public Relations Division of the Chief Executive's Department have been unfailingly helpful. But, above all, I wish to place on record my warm thanks to the security, design, technical, conservation curatorial and clerical staff of the City Museums and Art Galleries for their enormous hard work in connection with this project.

HERBERT COUTTS
City Curator

AUTHORS

Warwick Bray
Metalwork in pre-Hispanic Peru;
Bibliography

W. Iain Mackay

Cat. entries   12, 31-36, 115-121, 154-157,
162-163, 166, 251-260, 277,
290-300

Victoria Mujica de Pérez Palacio

Cat. entries   1-11, 13-30, 37-114, 122-153,
158-161, 164-165, 167-250, 261-276,
278-289

These entries were translated from Spanish by
S. Anita Schrader and W. Iain Mackay.
Further information was provided by Herbert Coutts
and W. Iain Mackay.

PHOTOGRAPHS

Junius Bird: Fig. 12
James Dallas: Figs. 11, 17; Cat. Nos. 12, 31-33, 35-36, 115-121, 154-157,
162-163, 166, 253-260, 290-296, 299

C. B. Donnan: Fig. 2

Stuart Laidlaw: Fig. 6

W. Iain Mackay: Fig. 18

Museo "Oro del Perú": Cat. Nos. 62, 139-153, 164-165, 195, 221-222,
226, 237, 240, 248, 250, 262-275

Alexander Topp: Figs. 1, 7, 8, 10, 13-16; Cat. Nos. 1-2, 9-11, 17, 19-22, 25,37,
41, 43, 49, 51, 63, 65-66, 74, 83-84, 86, 89, 92-101, 103-105,
107, 110-111, 123-124, 127-128, 131, 136, 158-161,
167-168, 170, 176-178, 181, 185, 187-188, 193, 203-204,
206, 220, 223-225, 242, 245, 261, 280-281

ILLUSTRATIONS

Ned Seidler (by courtesy of the National Geographic Society): Fig. 9
Carol Robertson: Back Cover
Stephen White: Map, Figs. 4, 5

GRAPHIC DESIGN

Stuart Adie

EDITOR

Herbert Coutts
© Copyright, City of Edinburgh Museums
and Art Galleries 1990.
Department of Recreation,
City of Edinburgh District Council.

Exhibition presented by

THE CITY OF EDINBURGH DISTRICT COUNCIL and the MUSEO "ORO DEL PERÚ",
under the auspices of the INSTITUTO NACIONAL DE CULTURA DEL PERU.
Media sponsor THE SCOTSMAN Official print sponsor NIMMOS COLOUR PRINTERS

Published by the City of Edinburgh Museums and Art Galleries, Department of Recreation,
City of Edinburgh District Council © 1990.
Design by the City of Edinburgh Museums and Art Galleries, Design Section. Printed by Nimmos Colour Printers,
Typeset by Impact Repro, Colour Separations by Marshall Thompson.